URBANSHEE

Urbanshee

poems by

Siaara Freeman

Button Publishing Inc.
Minneapolis
2022

URBANSHEE
POETRY
AUTHOR: SIAARA FREEMAN
COVER DESIGN: JESSI TOBIN

◇

◇

Published by Button Poetry
Minneapolis, MN 55418 | http://www.buttonpoetry.com

◇

Manufactured in the United States of America
PRINT ISBN: 978-1-63834-025-6
EBOOK ISBN: 978-1-63834-028-7
AUDIOBOOK ISBN: 978-1-63834-052-2

First printing

FOREWORD
By Rachel Wiley

I met Siaara Freeman in 2010 at a regional poetry slam.
She went by the stage name ControverSI. (the people deserve to know).

I was brand new to the game, and though she was very young she was not new.

I was impressed, intimidated, very nearly threatened by her boldness and her gravitationally charming presence.

Si and I were often the only woman on teams and in slams largely populated by men and there was a not-uncommon undercurrent meant to pit us against one another.

When I met Siaara I was only just beginning to learn that the other women in the room did not have to be my competition. That there could be, should be, and in fact always are more than one of us in the room; that we did not have to be ranked and divided for the entertainment of others.

My own chosen sister, Rachel McKibbens, showed me the strength in convening up and I have been fortunate enough to show my little sister what I have learned.

Like a true little sister she annoys me to no end, she has my back also to no end, and like a true big sister I refuse to leave her side.

Siaara is someone who has witnessed my becoming and unbecoming so many versions of myself and she has set down her Pepsi and embraced each one with finger snaps and tight hugs.

I have been fortunate enough to witness not only Siaara but also her writing flower from tightly gripped shock into choreographed awe.

This collection of Siaara's work almost makes me forget that time she somehow got blunt ashes in my lotion bottle. Almost.

This collection is a diligently mixed potion, a choose-her-own-adventure book, a yearbook, a book of spells, a dogeared headstone, a balm that shows you the beauty in your scars instead of disappearing them, a triptych of survival, a map to a secret mermaid cove, it is the price paid and it is priceless. It will not leave you empty handed as long as you show up with hands ready to receive, not to take.

Urbanshee

Age: The kind of old that keeps getting younger and younger
Sex: Only when she feels like it
Height: Taller than a grudge but shorter than regret
Weight: Of the entire goddammed world
Skin Color: If you have to ask you have never lived in it
Eye color: Black Black Black Black Black Black Black
Being: Bothered but blazed and highly favored

She crossed her legs outside her body & then she floated, unlike a
ghost & more like *I don't give a fuck.* She prayed over her loneliness,
until alone grew bright w/ sting & changed the definition to devotion
so she painted her fingernails that color & tried to scratch her eyes
out. I don't know if you are waiting to hear of her death but I won't
bring the news. Instead, I'll show you a map of a shipwreck, she is the
escape plan. I have agreed to lead you into the bleached woods, all
that you find to skin & eat is her honor. I hope you starve. Leave the
bones. I can show you her birthmarks, look up the titles of burned
books. You can sleep in her bald spots & all you ever have to do is
pay her some attention. Dandelions sprout where you hope she will
be. If you pluck one, you'd have to pluck three. What is left of her
hair, you can take & make into a baby blanket. You can ask about the
dead ducks but don't you be surprised when she starts to molt. If you
kiss her, you may wake up in a new religion. If you are afraid, she
will not beg for you not to be. You can turn her into a rumor or fill
her bed with ice & memory, Black as the day we were born of the
riddled man, of the crumbling nose. A woman soaked in *guess all you
want.* Please say what you will but remember she may come back to
bite you.

The myth is God took a smoke break & that's right when she decided
to happen. She will say the only truth is that
you can think whatever you like.

Contents

Chapter Four

Chapter Five

Chapter Six

Chapter Seven

URBANSHEE

Chapter One

Once Upon a Time on Loop

Lida **"Stony" Newsom:** *Y'all niggas done lost y'all mind.
We might as well not even talk about this shit no more.*
Francesca "Frankie" Sutton: *Well, I'm talkin' 'bout it.
And ain't nobody gon' stop me from talkin' 'bout it.*

—Set It Off (1996)

On Glorification

The sky is a dazzlingly selfish pair of child shoes,
shined w/ gum at the bottom. The hood is

all veiled bites & coiled jewels.
Grief & money run this

whole world. This whole world is a greasy wail. It stains whatever it
touches. It is always touching me. I'm not sure

my hood is not hate that has found greater
purpose. My love is a belligerent grunt

in the great kaput, a biting flag, the strangest loyalty.
Here is a seat

in my brain: it's covered in glow worms.
Do worms make you cry? Or curious? Or cruel

enough to cut them in half & see
if they can put themselves back together? That's how

I imagine my heart, my hood, my synapses: this quivering
slice of cranberry sauce on a very cheap, very loved plate.

It is a soothing suck of activity. Which sounds like a conversation that
becomes an argument where everyone is

right until they are wrong. When people ask me, *How can you
love a hood that took yo daddy,*

wicked fairy that I am, I read them
a new world where this poem is the sun.

World in Which the Word *Father* Is Replaced by *Hood*

Let me start by saying yes, I grew up w/ my hood
in my life. My hood loved me the moment I screamed

an ambulance quiet. My hood showed up to all major events
in my life & also the ones so tiny I only turn to them when I need

something else to forget. My hood thought my mama was ice water
& my hood often felt hell bound. When my mama & my hood danced,

my hood felt livable. My hood's a carnival of weed & wrong turns
& won't change its story, only its writers. My hood remains

both dead & alive, depending on what kind of God you got. Folks
be so quick to ask girls like me if our hoods loved us, if we had

hoods to begin with even, I know they want me to say more
about the drugs n' shit my hood was involved with; this

would make my hood easier to understand & dismiss. A hood
with nuance. They don't think of nuance when they think of Black

hoods, but audacity does not surprise me. My hood was murdered early
one April morning, or it might've been yesterday, really it could be soon

I visit my hood a lot & I won't lie, sometimes I cringe when I think of
how often that disenchanted path has had me stepping over my own

blood.

X Things They Never Tell You
About the Drug Dealer's Daughter

I. By the time she truly learns to love someone more than
    herself, he's already dead.

II. She is nine when she realizes she has the blessing of
    being brought up in this contemporary concept. She is the
    first on her block to get a stay-at-home dad. She brags:
    He plays Barbies & dominoes. My daddy can cook, y'all,
    we got enough baking soda in my basement to open up
    ten bakeries! The cakes they sell so fast I never see
    them—just the customers at the screen door lookin'
    some kind of hungry, like they got this sweet tooth only
    my daddy can snatch & I swear, y'all, we gon' be rich.

III. Her friends do not believe her until they all start turning
     training bra & things start disappearing & reappearing
     in her house: Tanya's television, Brandi's older brother's
     attention span. Danielle's uncle's four-fingered ring,
     Courtney's father's retirement fund. Brandi's whole
     mother.

IV. The girl, her father (the drug dealer), their family move to
    a new neighborhood. He (the drug dealer) (the father)
    don't miss the daughter's plays or her beauty pageants or
    her poetry slams & they aren't rich, but they aren't in
    those projects anymore, either.

V. By the time I realize what we are? It is already too late.
    We are an urban novel you will skim over at Walmart, a
    four-minute smirk on Fox 8's face, what would occur if
    Spike Lee & Quentin Tarantino produced a film under
    Eazy-E's direction. A question Black America asks itself
    every Sunday. I am a bakery with little sweet   left in it.

VI.   My father is killed. Shot point-blank range in the back of the left ear. Writing it down makes it more real, less legend, makes this poem more *ten things you did not know about Siaara Freeman,* less ten things about a cliché you can click your fucking teeth at.

VII.   Some nights I put on my father's chalk outline & I teach it how to walk. My face is a haunted house my mother screams at from habit, not fear. Most days I am an alley that no one should enter alone.

VIII.   My father is found with no jewelry, just a pocket watch w/ my baby teeth snuggled inside. After his autopsy, they are returned to me, chipped.

IX.   I disappeared into my old neighborhood. I had an itch, the suburbs don't got nails for. Danielle asks did I inherit any of my daddy's magic? I shake my head. She abracadabras a door into her arms and says, *You know the drug dealers deserve to die, right?*

X.   I know the stories, how the hood can turn many into myths & mythmakers. It is easiest to make monsters out of gods & Black men. Zeus made an exit wound big enough for his daughter to walk out of fully armored & Athena, unlike most goddesses, finally learned to love someone until she became more than herself.

Necromancy Explains the Author

When the girl speaks, all she asks is to be remembered or to
remember. Basically she has an undeniable urge to know what came
first: death

or prayer? She is luck kissed, a rabbit's foot with the trap still
attached. If you get near enough, you can smell the slow swarm of
devour, a skullfull of fire ants honeyed into a ballet

of repetitive nocturnal. She is not afraid of any hell she ain't help
create herself. The Blacker the manifestation, the redder the juice &
you know hoodrats got all the juice, you know they called us

spooks back in the day. A group of spooks was called a cemetery.
Don't start no séance, won't be no séance. What is she if not the
apparition's daughter. Her eyes are two graves, rolling.

The Author Explains Necromancy

When I speak of hunger I speak of ghosts. I speak of death easier said
than seen. A beehive, except all the bees

are bullets, except my father is a flower, I swear on a stack of bodies
stuffed together in a funeral limo that I am not alone in this. If you
think of them as ghosts, you will always

be afraid. If you think of them as alive, you will always be sad.
Regardless, you will think of them. It's not at all like being God, in
fact it's perfect proof that you would never be any good

at playing God.

I Wonder What Happens to the Little Black Girl from *Kill Bill Vol. 2*

what summons her to my mind? she deserves to be thought
about. same as my oldest sister. she is such a pretty girl. she has
one parent who was murdered violently, like mine. I suspect

> she has grown up to be a dark cave filled with churchless bells
> & *every right to want to get even.* I've heard too many people
casually ponder what they would do if they were her & I was, so for

> > > me, she is

Imp/possible not to consider. she is right there when I am
brushing my teeth, brushing her teeth too hard & creating
a garish pink print. she is raw skin with an itch you have

> to feel to believe. she plays too much. she plays too hard. she don't
> play well with others. she blames it all on a pet you never see. she
> laughs like glass underfoot, something spine cinching

& marks vengeance on the walls until it is my exact height. she
attends all my classes, but my students don't notice her, thank God.
Her hand stays up like a defense mechanism. I watch her hand

wave

> impatient as a red flag, until I am less teaching artist & more
> hostage. I don't call on her; I don't have any of the answers
> she needs. When I eat, she eats, so I am sure

> > > she is surviving

off fingernails & warm thoughts, ahh ambrosia. When I take my
medicine, she swallows for me. When she leaves, I am terrified
she will return content with a backpack full of butchered bones &

rationale what if I can't rinse the cereal & sinew from her
hair? so what if she is not my child, she still feels like my very own
dark responsibility. I imagine her fingers resemble mine if I had

picked up a gun. I think of the man who killed my father while she
knits a treasureless map until all four of our eyes fall out. I dream
of safety, she is there like a school bus, on time at the wrong

moment. every holiday I believe she pisses the bed; the next morning
my brain feels yellow. I know she hides snacks for later; sometimes
my thoughts are sticky. I know she has a plan. I just don't

want to know it. honestly, I know we both expect more from one
another instead of better because we are both too afraid to expect
better. We hold each other like strangers who know too

much. I want to protect her;
in the way you instinctually try
to catch yourself before

the fall.

Fair Is to Urban Girls

as luck is	to	a ghost
as light is	to	the grave
as begging is	to	the rich
as a prison is	to	the pumping blood
as joy is	to	a dreamless child
as a curse is	to	the willful witch
as a threat is	to	the immortal
as a sacrifice is	to	the spoilt
as a desert is	to	a siren
as a sphinx is	to	any backtalk
as a home is	to	the exiled
as the mirage is	to	a cleared mind
as silence is	to	glory
as hope is	to	the haunted
as harmony is	to	the harpies
as discovery is	to	the hunted
as human is	to	a changeling
as forgiveness is	to	the locked heart
as recall is	to	grace
as forgetting is	to	faith

Urban Girl in Four Non-Oscar-Nominated Parts
Part 1: There Is Always One
You Guess Won't Survive // T.T

The lamb is raised amongst lionesses, the lamb files her soft teeth
                              on old meat & fresh salt. Her
nature holds, but her hooves
                    sharpen. Her wool is still soft & cuddle ready,

however, you ought to be careful, you could easily find razors
                              or love or something else equally

unescapable. The lamb will play with the lionesses
                    & the lionesses, of course, will tease the lamb—

they have grown up w/ one another & have formed an alliance
                    from a caged life of untreated wounds & open-

mouthed stares. The lamb is just a lioness who knows
                              a kinder way. The lamb

eventually becomes a sheep. That's just how it is; someone has to

follow & soon no one believes she is not a lion
          or that she will not raise her lamb

around lions, or that she won't raise her lamb to be a lion. Simply put,
                              she is now considered
a danger to her offspring, which of course
          only makes her much more dangerous.

When the sheep is slaughtered, the lionesses will claw
                    her small body into an embrace

permanently staining their fur. Their roars will rot
                              into ghost howls & this is how

you make a whole new creature. Chew out a chunk of its heart & see
what is left. The blood is
                              all the same though, instinctually
                                                    in the wild
everything is
a sacrifice on loop.

Urban Girl in Four Non-Oscar-Nominated Parts
Part 2: Taking One Thing to Explain Another // Cleo

& all I'm saying is: Queen Latifa was the one
who decided to sacrifice herself in *Set It Off.* Cleo
w/ her beautiful fat & a laugh honey heavy, packs

of Newports strong. She died feeling disposable. You
shouldn't even have to live like that. Who decided to
sacrifice herself in *Set It Off*? Cleo w/ her beautiful fat

& a laugh honey heavy, packs of Newports strong. & all
I'm saying is, her scalp slipped back like an era. She died
feeling disposable. You shouldn't even have to live like that.

She not the only one to die, they all Black women, but of course
she is the first to offer. & all I'm saying is her scalp slipped back
like an era. Her girlfriend ain't speak the whole movie, a goodbye

caught in her throat like a wishbone. She not the only one to die, they
all Black women, but of course she is the first to offer. You can call it
what you want, but it is still a betrayal. Her girlfriend ain't speak

the whole movie, a goodbye caught in her throat like a wishbone.
Ursula a ghost to everyone except Cleo, I bet the first time she spoke
a haunting happened. You can call it what you want, but it is still

a betrayal. Heteronormativity often betrays itself, damn right it's gon'
betray you, sis. Meaning: when they ask what is different about this
picture & they will ask. You must point to yourself & disappear.

She open her pretty-ass mouth, I bet the first time she spoke a
haunting happened. '90s West Coast rap dripping like e'rrythang
shiny in the hood like bodies. Her friends pile up in her whip.

She love that mutherfucking car so much, I just know it's gon' be her
Casket, I know her girl gon' have to bury her alone. Meaning: I think
the most beautiful thing about *The Color Purple* is Shug & Celie

trying to kiss the ugly off each other & then realizing the ugly was
never theirs to begin with. Everything is
a sacrifice on loop.

Urban Girl in Four Non-Oscar-Nominated Parts
Part 3: *So, What's the Procedure When You Have a Gun to Your Head?* // Frankie

What's the fucking procedure
when you have a gun to your head?

Find a God to get closer to?
Or find a God to get further from?
Cry, but are all your tears sins then
memories? Do you say goodbye?
Or good riddance? Do you die a little
as practice? Does your piss have an escape
plan before you do? Do you curse & hope
that's not the last thing you ever fucking say?
Are you imagining a heaven for yourself
or a hell for them? Will something gnaw

its way out of you? Do you find a killer on the road
to self-preservation? Do you try & find a weapon? Do you
scream *help* or *run*? Is your brain shutting down? Can you
move? You try to barter? What will you trade your life for?
Is there any law that matters at this moment? Are you waiting
to be rescued? Who do you think is coming? Is it anyone

you love? Do you try to get on good terms
with your assailant? Do you ask them if they have kids?
Do you tell them about your kids? Even if you have to
make them up as you go along? Do you speak softly
Or are you firm of voice? Is it too hot

or too cold? Can you feel anything at all?
Is your breath gone? Like it is
already over? A sacrifice
on loop.

Urban Girl in Four Non-Oscar-Nominated Parts
Part 4: The One Who Gets Away // Stony

It's always at least one of us
who makes it out alive. We twerk

for her. We show you where she grew
up. Where she used to survive on

the same hustles we know.
Where she fucked around & got drunk

& fought w/ so & so, & slept w/ so & so, &
loves so & so. Tell you which blocks said she would

never leave. We go 'head & let you know how good
she doing. Glowing like a secret. Eating well.

Did something with herself. Did
something for herself. Did something for all of us. Girls

from the hood are always scarred, so this is sacred. This getaway
get godly. She the 4th way to Sunday. The only road towards rest.

We want to see her again, but at the same time
we hope she never come back. Maybe it did not get better but

she showl' did. We measure success only in how far we got
away. She smiles like she feels safe. She laughs

like she robbed a bank. Like there is so much she had to leave behind
& much more still she had to take w/ her. A miracle on any street.

We are told daily how we won't amount to anything. We point to this
girl & say *but maybe* on loop.

Chapter Two

Ancient like Darkness

The Witch: *Some things are better left unsaid.*
Aunt Mozelle: *I paid you a dollar, old woman. Now tell my fortune.*

—*Eve's Bayou (1997)*

Unfortunate

They are quick to tell you about the apple

        that does not fall far from the tree—

but what happens when the tree does not fall

        far from the apple? What happens

when the tree is chopped down not far

        from the apple? *I know what happens*

to the tree, it dies. What happens

        to the apple? What happens to the apple

when the eye it belonged to

        is no longer left to polish it?

Do not tell me the worms

        will smell the decaying core

and tunnel right through her.

        Do not tell me she is poisoned.

Do not tell me she keeps the doctor

away. She has become

a marijuana bong. She is peeling?

She is rotting from the inside

out. *Did anyone know this*

was going to happen?

Why wait so fucking long

to say something.

The (Urban) Urban Legend

For Jessica

Every time a Black girl in my hood is murdered,
the beauty shop becomes *who's next?* quiet.

A porch becomes a lifeboat. Ladies & children first.
The men cling to whatever they haven't destroyed in this

state of constant emergency. We huddle like a humming
pack of slaves, the names of the un-rescued chapping our lips.

Weed sales go up, but most of the corner boys just giving you
something for free or close. The corner girls are still comforting

survivors. Everybody say they was her cousin or friend or lover or
auntie or god-mama or classmate or neighbor or uncle or homegirl

or first kiss or last kiss or crush or worst ass whipping or co-worker or
got twerk from her at a house party once or got help on a math

test or owed 40 dollars or loaned 40 dollars or grace or grace or grace
& tomorrow was gon' see her. Or she looked damned

familiar. A Hennessy bottle is passed around, a lil bit of everywhere.
The liquor matches the amount of blood spilled from the Black

girl's body. The women & girls on the porch turn into creatures.
The creatures are made of many things but mostly scabs & laughter

& get up & go & come back when you can. They eat & drink & make
sure someone or something is full. The older ones

brush the younger ones' naps into merry scowls. The young ones
comb the older ones' scalps into well-worn maps. The creatures,

they have heavy skin of burning photographs, of themselves
screaming the murdered woman's name. The creatures wear gowns

& graveyard & lingerie & semi-automatics & Jordans & ridicule &
booty shorts & brass & knuckles & sundresses & grit & tuxedos

& glass & boxers & panties & strap-ons & nothing
can completely undress them. The creatures make a music

from their bones cause you to cry. Their eyes are each other & each
other & each other & each other & their jaws are denials revoked.

Their nails are anything they can throw that will stick. & that smile?
That smile? It is terror deciding

who to save first.

What's Understood Don't Have to Be

When I lit the blunt after my friend's funeral
no one was willing to call me
out about it.

No one said shit

like, *This a church,* or, *Have some respect.*
They knew me, knew that I needed a distraction,
wanted an argument more than I needed to get high.

Anyway. I blew rings that looked like halos.
My lungs burned like seven hells, each one I helped
make. Each one I barely escaped.

No Tradebacksies x ∞

TLC Poster for: a kiss from a girl who would lie about it today if you asked her.

A Kiss for: a Charizard card from a boy who died six weeks later because his pockets were empty.

Charizard Card for: an invite to a party that I would lie about today, right now if my mama asked me.

Invite to a Party for: invites to better parties, which I don't remember beyond the sweat & what it took to be there.

What It Took to Be There for: what it took to stay & what it took to leave.

What It Took to Leave for: Escape.

Escape for: an orgasm which was just a new word for escape.

Orgasm for: a pair of Jordans & the only time I really wanted to die.

Jordans for: my life, on the same street where the boy was found emptied.

Things I Learned in the Hood before Turning

Eight years old. Children do not speak, they listen to everything their parents do not catch coming out of they mouths. We pick up whatever dribbles over: spades, beer, curses, almost everything but love. Love does not dribble unless it has become something else entirely. I cup my hands & bottle my heart & beg for a spill I can clean up. I learn that being alone is good when you don't want anyone to touch you but also being alone is bad if you don't want anyone to touch you. I can wash myself & I can cook myself a small meal & I can play alone for hours. I learn to be capable. I can mostly take good care of myself. This is an easy way to learn how. I meet other girls from my hood & some of them have the hard way learned all in their face. My face is mostly questions & sometimes it an anxious concern. Years from now,

my therapist will say this may be the root of my people pleasing, but for now, I am not too young to know when not to ask questions, when the school bell rings & some of the other girls ask to spend the night. I know I have to beg for them to stay, I know I have never begged enough.

Haint Blue

Red, White, and Black Make Blue—Andrea Feeser

Grams says a haint sat on her bed when she was a girl. When I was a girl, I got to visit her childhood home where she learnt how to be the *third girl*. A lesson she taught my mama who taught me. Some thangs just got to be learnt on a porch. I am the third girl of a third girl of a third girl of old blood in a new body. I am a Freeman. I am love & craft & country. I got some steady eyes in the back of my hope. Some spells just take centuries & so much blood to complete. I be a good book in bad hands. I am the sword & the stone it was pulled from. I am pinned to my own chest like a note from a teacher. Education is a woman who comes from porch people. Ancient like

darkness. Each strand of her hair is a new name for a god that you won't even try to pronounce correctly. Her heart is on backwards. I am to go back & stop her from crossing the water. I am haunting myself for generations. I am haunting myself into myself into myself. The water is whatever you think it is. I am right after something borrowed. A gift that will not be returned easily.

Indigo child, my sister Angie called me indigo child when I was a child. I looked it up only once & it scared the prayers out of me. Just like in third grade when that lady with a smile filling the whole classroom sent me home with a packet. I read it before sharing it with my mom or my grandma. I couldn't stop shivering. It said, *Your child is terribly gifted*, it did not say with what.

Once You Know What Your Father's Brain Looks Like

outside his skull, you understand life better
than other 16-year-olds. Once you ask about open or closed
caskets, you are essentially at least 30, you have time to develop
an ulcer, you have already graduated high school a quarter
million times. You know exactly what love is now & you are suddenly
uninterested. When the coroner asks your age—you don't remember
your birthday—it's in two weeks—you tell him you're not sure,
but you know every second you are getting closer
to your father. You remember your grade—this room
reminds you of dissection, three weeks ago you squirmed
at the fetal pig's corpse, you had to be excused from class—
I'm a junior, you say. Your hands are steady as he pulls
the sheet back. He wants to know if you are ready.
You yank what is left of your father into view.
He explains how the bullet entered his skull.
You repeat him. He talks measurements & metal
& cartilage & you make sense of this despite
your brain being its own vicious assault. You refuse
to cringe. You spent the night before learning
new terminology. You can speak forensics, you can speak
autopsy, you are efficiently fluent in fatality.
The coroner makes eye contact with you after
you correctly identify the portion of your father's brain
most destroyed. He says, *Kid, sorry about your father, really, I am
but you might have a future in this.*

Coughing

When you were a child of six or seven, your mother had tuberculosis.
Your father, your two sisters, & you had to take medicine in order
not to also contract it. When you prayed, you prayed hard

for all of them, especially your mother, but never you. You believed
you were only supposed to pray for good people; you knew you could
not say for sure you were one. You knew how bad

you just wanted to go & play outside, how the whole fucking house reeked
of coughed blood. You knew somehow that this was only the start of swallowing
the things you would have to go to God about.

On the Day I Learned My Father Was Murdered, I Learned

My mother is a person. A real one.
Not just a mom person, not just endless
love, not just mine.

Not just someone to share
with my sisters, not only a heart to nest
in, an entire being & one who deserved

a vacation or an empire. It sounds strange,
but I was sixteen & had no idea who I was
living with. I had a short list: her love is

unconditional & she works double shifts
as a wound care nurse & can dance the dusk down.
She makes me laugh & teaches me how to curse

under my breath occasionally. Listen, my dad is dead
& I am in the backseat of my grandparents' car trying
to explain what I had never before considered possible.

I have already fucked up, which is a great head start
to early adulthood—turns out there is no good way
to say *Dad was murdered*

early this morning. I tell one sister & she faints
quickly after. I tell my other sister who is five months pregnant
& everyone around me feels delicate & full of tomorrow

& I feel like a last night forever emptying
into one long wish. My mother will leave her job smiling, she will
see her parents' faces & know something is wrong. First,

she demands to know where both my sisters are; I manage,
They're safe, & without warning she immediately knows
someone is not. I tell her & the words crack a window

in my throat that I will never replace. When the words leave
my mouth, I know I have committed a terrible crime. Her face
breaks like a thousand plans. Plans, I had no idea

even existed.

Urban Girl Finally Responds to the *Yo Mama* Jokes

My mama SO strong—a hurricane named its kids after hers

My mama SO much pressure—she made three diamonds in 39 years

My mama SO smooth—she talk like her skin

My mama SO smart—she became my mama

My mama SO Black—America don't know whether to kill her or clone her

My mama SO hood—if you GPS *survival* you end up in her arms

My mama SO majik—unicorns chose not to exist when they heard she was coming

My mama SO old—she could teach you something

My mama SO Black—you sit her next to God & you can barely tell the difference

My mama SO holy—duh, my daddy is a ghost

My mama SO bougie—she taught me not to talk about other folks' mamas

My mama SO Midwest—she said, Bless your heart & meant, Fuck you

My mama SO fly—she got birds embarrassed

My mama SO pretty—she make flowers shy

My mama SO loud—the devil shhhhhhhhhhhhhhhhhhhhh

My mama SO fat—yo' wallet is jealous

My mama SO soft—yo' edges is jealous

My mama SO poor—she give her three daughters everything she got

My mama SO Black—she give her three daughters everything she got

My mama SO hood—she give her three daughters everything she got

My mama SO nosy—she kept me alive

Haint Green

i. A funny thing happened at my father's funeral. His friend owed him
   money & he put it in the coffin with him. My father was a Capricorn.

   The joke was he couldn't rest. Or maybe the joke was he wouldn't rest.

   Or maybe the joke was rest. Rest, lol, can you imagine?

ii. What would you take with you if it turns out we can take something
    to somewhere? A secret? A picture of your mother, her eyes bright
    with yesterday? An ice cream sandwich? A book of poems you have
    to learn to love?

iii. The punchline is unfinished business. No other way when one is
     murdered. In that church pew, Valium held me like a hero as I watched
     the whole thing through eyes everyone calls his. A man walks into
     heaven then suddenly remembers he left his spitting image.
     He realizes he has her smile in his right hand, he looks down
     (despite the warning). I knew he would.

iv. Ever laugh so hard your eyes water down the ghosts?

v. Ever ghost so hard you water down your laughter then your eyes?

vi. After the funeral, I see him everywhere. Every time a man is shot
    in the head. I see him between the couch cushions. The blunt's end,
    in Jamaica drinking a Red Stripe on a patch of grass, in a backyard drunk
    with witches dancing to Motown. Screaming from my mouth. In
    my lupus diagnosis. Laying in the cracks of my knuckles. Knock, knock,

    who's there?

vii. What is dark humor? A woman snipping then discarding the bloom
from a rose, caressing the thorns & admiring what brings the blood?
A woman gets on stage, tells her story, & decides the audience needs

to be more comfortable; she pretends her pain is relatable. At night it is not enough & coin-sized patches appear on her scalp, so she spends hours in the mirror attending tiny funerals, trying to laugh his face off.

In Attempts to Bring You Back

I found the last thing you ate & saved it. Idc.
Idc. Idc. Even when the flies came, I simply
introduced myself to the rot. We sat there

> for hours reminiscing about being something sweet
> in this war left to spoil, we sang *Suga*
> *On The Flo* pretending we could not smell one another

out of kindness. I begged it to become you.
It begged me to finish it. We both eventually
gave up; it went to the trash, & I went to college

> like we discussed in our last conversation. Then I quit
> school like seven times to see if that would make you mad enough
> to return. You didn't. Resentment swayed through, so I drowned her

& demanded this be seen as sacrifice. Then I became a candle.
Then I melted. Then I waited for you some more. Then I began
thinking my plan was better than God's,

> then I realized I had been begging God to be a god,
> & thus I had to beg God to forgive me for asking. I thought
> about having a child, naming it after you. Then I realized that child

would never know its namesake & that it's not fair
to want someone just because you want someone else. Instead
I named other things for you: seasons with the most holidays,

> the sky's face seven seconds before or after
> it hails, the sound a heart hears when it is half returned, the first time I
> won a fight, anytime I lose anything. The smell a bullet leaves

on a person—even when they aren't the target. I drew a circle
in the middle of the last block you walked. I summoned
a banshee & I maintained eye contact.

I needed to know why I wasn't warned. I offered. I threatened.
I bargained & the banshee wasn't even surprised to see me there.
I am the talk of the afterlife after all, a joke

the myths tell: *silly human who imagines*
she has something the darkness has not seen before.

Chapter Three

A Library of Alchemy

he asked me could I read and write. I told her,
Of course, and I can talk too.
　　　　　　—Sister Souljah, *The Coldest Winter Ever (1999)*

Urban Girl

After Terrance Hayes, Angel Nafis, & Natasha "T" Miller

Urban Girl/Urban area/Urban Girl is her area. Urban Girl bad
investment, not safe for children, quick depreciation in value,
eviction. Urban Girl (un)noticed, (un)speakable property

damaged. Most folks act surprised
that Urban Girl is even able to speak. Urban Girl get spoke at,
spoke wit, spoke for, spoke through but not to. Never to.

Urban Girl get cat-
called also, 'cept y'all say Urban Girl deserve it—always
dressed like it, Urban Girl is fast, Urban Girl got a child & a hood,

but Urban Girl don't got no childhood.

Y'all got jokes. Y'all funny
acting. Urban Girl gets jokes. Urban Girls gets murdered
daddies, murdered mamas, murdered brothers, murdered sisters,

murdered cousins, murdered aunties, murdered
uncles, murdered friends, murdered lovers.
Urban Girl heard you say death is natural. She used to seeing it

with her own blood on them streets. Urban Girl make a whole
language out of family & blood & streets. She know
you won't understand.

Urban Girl know YOU say *urban*
when what you really want to say is *ghetto,*
& you do. You say, *It's the ghetto.* You don't care

who calls it home.
Urban Girl heard you. She knows what condescending feels like.
Fuck if she can spell it. Urban Girl spells it. Urban Girl turned her

hand into an answering
machine in the '90s so you may speak to it. Urban Girl '90s.
Urban Girl BeBe & BeBe's kids proof of the we don't die

we multiply equation.
Urban Girl dead daddy ghost grin
right from her face: talk to the hand!

Urban Girl answer y'all whether y'all like it or not. She leads the line
from the back. Urban Girl has stood in line
for Jordans. Urban Girl has stood in line for shit

she don't want all the time
anyways. Urban Girl: Free Lunch: Care Source: Public Assistance.
Urban Girl hide her everything

in her eyes. She bets it's the one place y'all won't look
for too long. Urban Girl saw you write *welfare queen*.
Urban Girl dyslexic. Urban Girl reads: farewell queen

or fare well queen or fair wail queen.
Urban Girl always understands she's a queen tho.
She more *Empire* than *Scandal*.

More Cookie than Olivia.
Don't understand why y'all think Ms. Pope got it
soooooo much fucking better.

Urban Girl will *Set It Off* up in here.
Urban Girl: Stony: Cleo: Frankie: T.T, Urban Girl
Jada Pinket Smith: Queen Latifa: Vivica A Foxx: Kimberly Elise—

Urban Girls make you say they whole name;
fuck if you can't spell it, you can feel it. Urban Girl make you
feel it. Urban Girl know you a copycat

& that you grimy with it. Urban Girl saw
you twerking. Heard you call Miley innovative & then say Rhianna
real ratchet. Urban Girl gets it. LOL

YOU alternative & Urban Girl yo' bad example?
Urban Girl still yo' example. Urban Girl still bad.
She don't need yo' praises. She want

all her roses black if you gon' give 'em. She knows
the concrete they come from. She bets
if they red, they might've been bleeding.

Urban Girl murdered roses. Urban Girl used to it; Urban Girl old-
skool. Urban Girl: all my life I had to fight. Urban Girl old-
skool. Urban Girl sphinxspeak. Urban Girl smarter than you

think. She a lion's jaw of riddle & bones.
She get her story told in shade. In every shade
but her own. Y'all so shady.

Urban Girl get her nose knocked off. Still draped in gold. Still.
Standing. Urban Girl still standing draped in gold.
Still standing all this time.

Still standing.
Still standing. Still
giving muffacas something to awe about.

How Cleopatra Must Have Felt in Rome

"don't save her, she don't want to be saved, don't save her"—Project Pat

It is said in a whisper that is only a whisper
in concept. I can hear them & they know it.
Tilting their heads behind the goblets I gifted
them.

Their smiles are small white children who have
never been scolded or taught to say thank you
or taught to dance. I can hear them & they know
it. The uncomfortable laugh after blood,

the washing of hands, the comfortable laugh
after blood. Crocodiles flourishing as lily pads.
They say I let the night curl up my eyelids, make
moons where there should be none,

who would not mistake me for the sky & prey? Pity
the fool who sees goddess where there is nothing
but whore. Pity the soul who sees queen where
there is nothing but desert & girl & spice & panic

& gold & lust & gold & gold & empty & empty &
empty & panic & surrender running through her
long wet untapped. They talk about my parents
like I am not in the room.

They say I was raised by the dead in a harem,
a brothel baby. All the riches I flaunt & I am still
half-naked/half-wit. They say to hail from a land
where they kill their own people, I am

a most charming savage. A festering time
capsule they have pried open & open & open but do not
value. They say I had my children for their government's
assistance, that I multiply

like a wanton goat, that they will kill anything I produce
& call royal before the bastards can inherit their futures.
They say do not save me. Pity the fool who tries to
save me. I don't want to be

saved. They say, *Dance, we want to see you dance. The whole
world is talking about it, we want to watch up close as we can
without tripping the curse on the tomb.* They call me *a library
of alchemy shaped like a cast spell;*

they say, *Pity the fool who runs & hides
in the dangerous, dangerous black.*
They swear they will never stop
talking about me

Alternative Descriptions for Hoodrats

After Danez Smith

A bird avoiding the land lines that hope to cut its throat;
venom-filled creature spilling itself

in bites. A phone call you either ignore or answer way too fast
or way too late. A prayer cut to the bone.

A song you love but you don't know any
of the words to. The rapper you hate but would still sleep with.

A cold razor beneath the crouching tongue. The Vaselined face,
ponytail as a sign of war. Smells of burning

hair & marijuana. A disappearing act with no audience. OR
the audience is ashamed to be there

OR the audience is happy
to be there but won't tell its friends & family OR the audience is all

ghosts. A robbed grave. A library, ablaze, seduced by the smell
of its own smoke. Slum Queen/The Coldest

Winter Ever/Dirty Red/Flyy Girl/Pay Back with Yo Life/A Project
Chick/A Project Chick 2/Girls

from the Hood Vol. 7/Sheisty/
Still Sheisty/Nervous/Addicted/True to the Game/Black Girl Lost/

The Family Business/A Ghetto Love Story/The Cartel/Justify My
Thug/Dirty Money/The Prada

Plan/Bitch/The Streets Have No King/Whoreson/Kiss Kiss, Bang
Bang/A Gangster's Girl/Forever

a Hustler's Wife/A Deeper Love/
Charge It to The Game/Skeezers/Treason/War/Prison Throne/The

House That Crack Built/Luxury Tax/Hoetic Justice/Pitbulls in a Skirt/
Level Up/The Streets Have

No Mercy/Trust No Man/Don't Blink/The Day the Streets Stood Still/
A swamp-

less crocodile. Nile-less
queen. The cocaine baptism. No home training. No home country,

just a street, only a block, maybe miles if you measure in blood.
An unpaid bill. Reason

to acquit. A waste
of resources, but so resourceful. A curse on all your houses

Me/me/me/me/m/me/me/me/me//me/me/me/me/me/me/me/
Me/me/me/me/me/

me/me/me/dead
OR alive.

The Girl Is from the Hood

This makes her a _____

low
murmur no matter where she goes. She thinks
about where she grew up & how easy it was
before the threads were cut

slowly into thinner threads, until everything could fit
right through her. She was a shiny pointed needle
in a stack of pointier needles. There is no hay

in her story, hay is for girls who land softly,
for distraught corn silk maidens & their glazed sky,
blue checkered dresses & their tiny dogs bred for baskets

& their heartless/brainless/spineless companions, certainly not
for the girl from the hood the jailed queen pin
cushion & her large heart bred for

their baskets & her breathless/breathless/breathless
companions. The girl is from the hood & this makes her
ruby slippers mean something else—makes her

watching the melt a painful thing. Where is the triumph
in watching the dead die? Who is a man who grants wishes
but a man who hides behind praise?

The girl is from the hood. We all heard the rumor
that someone is hanging, life heavy from a thin thread in her
background but who *really* paused long enough to check?

We Know It's Rude to Ask

For Amber Rose

They squint at you like they used to squint at my great
grandmother Carrie, unsure if you can say nigga or not.
You look like us in the right dark.

They know you a hoe

in somebody's dirt. They know the dirt is Black. They sure
the dirt is Black. Nigga has a home in the dirt. They knew
about y'all fruit. They got a home in the nigga.

They got a home in the dirt. Got a home in the black

dirt, nigga. They stare long & hard at you, like therapy
miss. They know it is rude to ask you what you are, but
they think it's rude that you won't

mention. When you got left for a white woman,

all of them shook
they heads. Pendulums of time & time again.
When you got left for a white woman, they said,

You got left for a white woman,

so then they said, *maybe,* & when that Black man said he had to
shower you from his body before entering his white wife, whew,
chile, they gathered you in they eyes

& could not blink you out
& they said, *Lord help her,*

maybe she is
one of us.

Self-Made

Kylie Jenner is watching television in my bedroom, watching *The Wiz* & she is jumping on my bed. She secretly wants to know why there is not more than one white person in *The Wiz,* but she is smart enough to know she should not ask. I look in my room really well & see things are absent. Important things **are** missing. My things. The walls are white & barren & laughing in the spaces my things were. I ask her where my things are. Kylie is honest, she mutes *The Wiz,* looks me where my face *was* (it is barren & white & laughing now.) Kylie say she gave it all away. That it is American. All of it. My room is music-less & dance-less & the maps are missing an entire continent. It is everything they've always wanted. It is *everything:* The "Juice." Jherri Curl drool. The spit the brown mother takes on finger to wipe faces clean of dirt, of tears, of shame, of joy. Shug Avery piss. WAP. Kylie Jenner is *still* on my bed, attempting to take her cornrows out. She is ready for something new. Every time she takes one down, a different one appears. Simple Kylie Jenner, she did not know cornrows were created as protection. Kylie Jenner is getting very tired & the cornrows will not stop multiplying. She tries to talk but her lips swell like a bloody history. Her lips bloom like opaque magnolias & suddenly no one hears her. She finally sounds Black enough to be silenced. She looks me in the barren-white-laughing face she has traded for my own sobbing brown & asks for help &

_____

no one answers.

The Reclaiming

The hood can yell for itself. The hood does not need
                              your voice to introduce its own,
                  your quick mimic, it is a quiet crime
                              & a loud sentencing. This dialect,

our Ebonics is not a case study nor a thesis
                              statement. It ain't no sociology report. Not
                                                            a buffet
nor a welcome mat.

                              Your children have full mouths
              of my children & you call this *rebellion* instead of *theft*
                              because rebellion looks better with blood.
You can learn every dance & you will never know
                  the sweat of needing to move with nowhere to go.
You can listen to every rap song & you will never live
                              the lyric, be the drug deal gone

good, be the love story gone bad,

                                                            be the shit

talk, be a barbeque of good intentions. You can come
                  to the house parties & go
home before the song ends, before the cops come, before
                  you actually have to understand everything important.
You can recite every line to *Friday* & never laugh
                              at the right parts. You can say, *Bye, Felicia,*
without knowing her
                              crack addiction. Without knowing
the droop of her shirt & the beg of her
    braids. How love & shame can be sisters & still look nothing alike.
                                                            How
hungry is always around the corner. Where survival comes

without the guide or loses it too soon.
You can be the Huxtables

or the Bradys—either way
you don't know a damn thing about this. Who you know
hiss like a hot comb

on the back of yo neck? Who you know *really*

trappin'? Who you know
really trapped? Watchu know 'bout reckless?
Who you know *really*

wrecked with no insurance? Who you know
ridin' dirty? Who you calling
dirty? Who

you won't bring home to yo mama? Who you think
you foolin'? Who you think a fool? Survival is a sticky sap. Slang is
what happens when we eat it

every day & wake to lick the corners
of our lips. *Our children play together,*   you sneer,
picking up your children's bad habits. You convince them

they eating dirt instead of warning
them to stop
taking
candy
from strangers.

The OUTside & the INside of the Joke

The OUTside (of) the Joke

BYE FELICIA BYE FELICIA BYE FELICIA B

	The Inside (of) the Joke	
Y		Y
E		E
F	Felicia has no job to speak	F
E	of. She has a part tho right	E
L	down the middle of her head.	L
I	Like someone tried to cut her	I
C	open & half her. She scratches	C
I	like a screen door left open	I
A	all summer, her tongue is a red	A
B	carpet for flies. She was	B
Y	born with a burning spoon	Y
E	in her mouth. She's a river	E
B	with bloody lips. Infection	B
Y	lurking beneath a Band-Aid.	Y
E		E

BYE FELICIA BYE FELICIA BYE FELICIA

The Outside (of) the Joke

aiN'T gOT NO JOB AiN't goT No jOb ain'T GoT <u>NO</u> ~~JOB~~

	The Inside (of) the Joke	
I		A
N	Tommy don't got no job.	I
'	He still kicking it tho, still	N
T	got jokes. He got just enough to take	'
G	Pam out. He has just enough for you	T
O	to wonder how he got it,	G
T	smooth & Black as he is. Smooth	O
N	just like my daddy, just like a drug dealer, just like	T
O	an iced highway, a death that only comes in bright	N
J	reds. Loud deaths. Ones that make you	O
O	wonder who they were before everyone starts talking bout how	J
B	they died.	O

aiN'T gOT NO JOB AiN't goT No jOb ain'T GoT <u>NO</u> ~~JOB~~

The Outside (of) the Joke
HoW yOu LoSe Yo JoB oN yO DaY oFf H

O	**The Inside (of) the Joke**	O
W		W
Y	How you lose yo job	Y
O	on yo day off? Lordt,	O
U	that is some nigga	U
L	shit right there, bruh!	L
O	Guess it's 'bout that time	O
S	to get high, homie. You	S
E	ain't got shit else	E
Y	to do. You still living	Y
O	in yo mama's house?	O
J	Still eating	J
O	all the hog mogs?	O
B	You need some	B
O	money? Who you	O
N	owe? Heard yo dawg	N
Y	got his shit laced. You put down	Y
O	the gun then just as quick	O
D	picked up a brick.	D
A	**OK, nigga, but did you**	A
Y	**die?**	Y

hOW YOu LOsE yO jOb On yo DAy oFf

The Outside (of) the Joke

JAZZ GE~~TS~~ ~~TOSSED~~ ~~OUT~~ JAZZ GETS TOSSE~~D~~ OUT

A	The Inside(of) the Joke	*J*
Z	Jazz gets kicked out	*A*
Z	the Banks	*Z*
G	residence. Hillary Banks is too good	*Z*
E	for him. She is the kind of	*G*
T	Black that makes white people	*E*
S	feel safer. Jazz is the kind of Black	*T*
T	that causes white people to create laws	*S*
O	to break in order	*T*
S	to get rid of him. Judge	*O*
S	Banks is the kind of Black that feels	*S*
E	superior when it can	*S*
D	throw out its alleged trash	*E*
O	for the white people	*D*
U	to recycle.	*O*

J~~AZZ~~ GE~~TS~~ ~~TOSSED~~ OUT JAZZ GE~~TS~~ ~~TOSSED~~ OU~~T~~

& this is how
it works,
the laughs
separated

by a thin smile.   The moment

when you're not   sure what is
so funny.

But you   can't stop

laughing,   tears streaming
down   your brown face,
saying,   *Fam, fam,*
I am hollering,,

I am yelping,
                                                                    I am screaming,
I am
                                                                    dying.

Urban Girl Bonds With:

Barbed Wire

Who had you twisted first? Was it a man
from Ohio? Were you a weapon forged
in a harsh environment? What are you
keeping out? What did you let in before
      that made you one long drink
          of blood?

Lake Erie

It calls her by a name she buried
in its mouth & what a dirty mouth
that speaks of floating & how much
it looks like death & how much she knows
about both.

Winter Santiaga

Black & hood & rich & hood-rich
& daddy sell dope—& e'rrybody stay talking
'bout how yo mama & you & yo sistas always so fly
—& when they kill yo daddy, keep yo head skywards
like it's always been in a noose. Like you always been
waiting on the right kick.

Marijuana

I'm still illegal in plenty of places
in America, too. People do me & call me
a problem in public. Once I was scared—
I had been passed around so quickly
nothing was left but ashes.

Bobbi Kristina

I wanted to die like my father, a reenactment
of the moment that changed everything. Wanted a walk
in his headline. To be the reaction un-delayed. I wanted
to tell you in case you are with her now & *I understand*
still means anything.

Urban Girl Finds:

Joy

without stealing it. She finds it
in places most ain't willing to go. She
run wild, they called her fast & she took it
like a misplaced compliment. Urban girl
an old doorbell, bronzed/weather-beaten
but still full of a bright rusted song.

A Penny

It's tarnished. Made in the '90s
just like she was. Government couldn't
keep its hands on her either. Picks it up
without knowing if it's lucky. All she knows
is: it does not deserve to be left on the ground.

A Way Out

The Hood	A Backseat	A Fight
The Salon	A Country	A Prison
The Corner Store	A Date	A Lie
The Past	A Body	A Curse

Yo Mouth

Chapter Four

A Name She Buried

The loss pressed down on her chest and came up into her throat. It was a fine cry—loud and long—but it had no bottom and it had no top, just circles and circles of sorrow.|
—Toni Morrison, *Sula (1973)*

Haint Black

It's the most southern shade of Black known
to God. You stare too long & it get to looking
like blood. It's dark as niggas long gone.

Crayola tried to make a crayon, but it kept
disappearing from every box it was placed in. Guess
it wasn't to be sold. Or lost & forgotten.

The first séance was this color. The last slave
will be this color. Can't find no land that don't know
its face, fate, or fatality.

Some nights
I close my eyes
& it is all I see.

The Part of the Story I Failed to Mention

The boy & I sit across from each other.

I have been seventeen for the last twelve days.
Seventeen is a fatherless job.
I am trying to get fired.

The boy is fourteen & already looks
so much like his father I can imagine him
killing mine.

I am not afraid of him or his death
promise hands that twitch like they need
a gun to feel free.

Our fathers' lawyers have us
positioned in the courtroom so that the jury
must face us. We must devastate

the jury. His father's freedom depends on it.
My family's justice depends on it. His father
gives him a soft smile from his seat.

My father gives me a grainy smile
from his obituary. The boy heavily steps
to the stand, stares at me, & states:

*I know that my father shooting her father
in the head was wrong, but I still need
my father.*

When it is my turn, I step to the stand
& I stare up at God & scream: *I still need
my daddy, I still need my daddy, I still need*

my daddy & on that day & never again
has being defeated worked
in my best interest.

Meet You At The Crossroads (Erasure)

tell
me   When

there ain't no   run
(tell me what)
        & whatcha gonna do   ain't no
hide
(tell me what)
judgment comes for you
come for   it Little boo.

God's
my gang. look to   lay   with
        me to say
        please Bury me
grand-grand

&   God bless you workin' on a
plan to heaven
        Praise   all up in my face
            Grace for the   race
with chance   my soul
        there's mercy for thugs
it's all about our family   Can I get a
let it unfold

We livin' our lives to eternal our soul aye   aye   Pray, &
pray &   pray, &   pray, &   pray Everyday, everyday,
everyday, everyday   pray,   pray,   pray,
pray still   tell of
            people that's long gone.

Exactly how many   we got lastin'

laughin'   away   rest

I know I'ma meet you up at the crossroads

know y'all forever   from them bone   s baby

Eazy's long gone   wish   home

when it's time to die

cry, cry Why they kill my

y'all   What they did

was wrong   so wrong, oh so wrong Gotta hold on

gotta stay strong   Better believe

you can lean on   we

&   pray, &   pray, &   pray Everyday, everyday,

everyday, everyday

you at the

crossroads,   you won't be lonely See

you at the crossroads,   So you won't be

lonely   you won't be

lonely

I'm gonna miss everybody   when

I'm gone & I'm gonna

Livin' in a

world sendin' me straight to heaven

& I'm askin' the

murder y'all,

Can somebody anybody tell me why? Hey, can

anybody tell me

I don't wanna die ▮ so wrong ▮ Oh, so wrong ▮
wrong. ▮
▮
▮
▮ at the crossroads
▮ See you at the cross▮
you won't be lonely. See ▮ the ▮roads, ▮
▮ See ▮
▮ So you won't be lonely .

So you ▮ S▮ o▮ a▮ r ▮

Paranoia

I knew this was going to happen.
They called me crazy 'cause they couldn't fit *right* & *woman*
in the same mouth. My friend was shot & left on the train tracks, her
heart one last roar & I can't help but think of how they never did find
little Shakira Johnson. That summer my mother treated outside like
the plague it could be. The police never did look for her like they did
JonBenét. Ohio is known for producing a large amount of serial
killers & a hoard of hauntings. We have a Cleveland Remembrance
page on Instagram where hood niggas mourn daily or just pretend
they are detectives. I admit I check it every morning, yes I know

a broken block can be correct
at least twice a day. I have this terrible dream that I call the cops &
instead they send an ice cream truck but all the photos of sweets are
replaced with the faces of the dead & a voice I've never heard before
screams, *CHOOSE CHOOSE CHOOSE CHOOSE CHOOSE*

I pace. I say *safe*
& it sounds like *please*. I pace. I say *please* & it sounds like I am
being dramatic. I say Ariel Castro. I say ten fucking years. I say
Anthony Sowell. I say eleven fucking women. People still say *who?*
They look at me, with they nerve & say *paranoid*. I point to a grave

& say *not there*

Grinding

My father is gone, but one of his friends still asks
me what he would think if he could see me on this stage shaking
my ass, like the whores they used to throw bills at. I don't need
a degree to know he is really asking: what if my father could see him
watching me shake my ass tonight? I think
my father would be angry either way, so I say, *Yes, he would be mad.*
This calms him, looks like he figured I would be ready to argue him
down about it, to release some of the tension that had throbbed him

into approaching me. I don't back away,
I don't charge him for the guilt, it's free in the club, dribbling out of
lips & into laps. It's not the guilt that keeps him here, or my father
& his ghost, a fearsome saint with one bullet shot to the head. It is

the G-string slicing my ass like a warm
muffin, licks the corner of his mouth like it's a street he wants
to clean. He sees the sweat sliding between my tits & dreams
of a river he can drown in. His dick is aimed at me like a lesson

I am supposed to learn. He looks the same
ashamed he wants me to feel. I dance on him all night.
I leave him penniless & apologizing to a dead man.

We Said *I Love You,* But I Think We Were Both Trying To Get the Last Word

You are a belt.
Not sure if you're helping
to keep me up or down.
My heart sags
like the delinquent's
God. A crocodile
saw me one night
& decided to grow
teeth. You winked
& I became
an emergency room
full of children
with the exact same fever.
You asked if I could take it.
When I couldn't,
you told me
you had a girlfriend
that you loved.
You asked,
What was the point
of leaving home
for the wild
if the wild also
wanted a picket fence?
I rolled over
& watched
the last six months
of *our* life dim
to a gray. I would be lying
if I said I did not try
to take it. I would be lying
if I said I did not wish
myself a prison, each time
you entered me.

Urbanshee Predicts the Birth of Toni Morrison & Writes Her a Letter

I see you sis & I smile a lonely summer until the sun skims

my skin like a softly wooded creek. Your light rippled

like anything heavy & meaningful will if given enough space

& the space you made felt like God's gap. Black & lawless like

dark roads winding through Ohio. I married myself once & no one

was there, Toni. No one gave me away. I did it alone in night-fulls,

sorrow drunk & high off another day's regret just waiting for the wind

to laugh lightning bugs from all directions swarming to form a person

size jar that you know I gladly stepped in. The bugs remembered that

I never once forgot to leave holes for air & so they returned the favor

the light licked me cleaner glimmering bones & a gown stitched in

haint skin. I pulled the future over my body & let the snug turn to

hymn. The hymn turned to feathers so there I was molting on a

disappearing bridge when my hymen broke. Your name rushed from

my lips as a flooding river. There wasn't any blood I couldn't find use

for. I went to Eve's bayou. I learned to spot snakes with flowers in

their mouths. I made crowns of seaweed & learned the gossip of dead kingdoms & refused to die out without leaving something behind.

I wanted children so bad, once I grew woods silent for a week.

Bluebells fancied themselves friends of mine. Fungi leached bruised

milk from each breast. My nipples swole like leftover hearts. I want to

tell you I birthed something truly exquisite. A hummingbird

with a jeweled song. Two scaleless dragons with smiles that leap

like well-loved children. A sphinx so dark she had no choice but to

become the riddle. A siren's song offkey & kinder for it. Midwest

afternoons on a muddy bank raining gritty memories. I named them

all after you.

In February 1971, a woman plummeted from the balcony of the Chelsea Hotel, crashing to Earth eight stories below. In a lot of ways, this was the perfect ending for a woman who lived a consummate rock 'n roll lifestyle.
—Rocks Off *Magazine*

I Wish I Could Have Kissed Devon Wilson on the Mouth

Not to taste

Jimi Hendrix or Miles Davis
or Mick Jagger,
but to swallow her tongue
before she did.
Blade licker to blade licker,
I bet she tasted
like hallucination. I think
I see her
in my lover's wet cave,
listening for rain.
If I had been born earlier,
maybe if she had preferred poets
to musicians, belladonna to foxglove,
she would have chosen me, perhaps. It is so
very clear she wasn't the medicine, but she was
the mortar. Who you wanted to hold

the balm.

Death is the only fountain of youth;
coin fed, greedy & shrinking
the closer you get to God. Devon
with the afro heaven high. Devon
who knew banishment & wasn't bashful
about it. *A childhood characterized by
violence & poverty.* Leather-clad cocaine
cocktail; conversation

in the back of my throat.

She makes my heart water. I don't
understand how they could call her
a groupie & not what happens to the sweet
& mysterious black space after
the stars burn inside of it.
It's Devon,
not quite divine but kinda
close. I know the feeling
& I still wonder what it tastes like
on someone else. & I know it's irony
because this is what she was
doing her whole entire
legend. So starved
That when hope came
she knew nothing

but to gulp it down.

& in the end no one knows
if she jumped or if she was pushed,
but she was certainly returned
to the concrete, replanted rose, her body
—a bloody bouquet
her audience—forever
ungrateful

The One Night

Stand & sometimes that is all
we are: an accumulation
of what others did not

need,

& how am I going to live
like that, off another's hard

earned indifference?

What if there is more to
me than a place
you run

to when you are cold

inside? What if I was

nothing but that—
doesn't that still make me
somewhere you were seeking

comfort?

What Had Happened Was

After Tracy Ameens "The Day Jazz Crawled Out"

A colored gal went & got
married to a river. It was said
it was the only one who would have
her. No shame in it, she was kind
& so forgave herself this muddy life.
When folks averted their eyes, she grew
even more unacceptable. Her hair started
making noise at obscene hours, waking
the dead & adding to their complaints.
She flashed her sorrows to townspeople & thus
they became ravenous, sensual, her hips swung
by tragedy's steady arms. She's been called out
her name so much that now she only answers
to abandon. She sang her own wedding song,
if you know the words, you have my sincerest
condolences. She borrowed faith & kept it so long,
it hers still. You've never met a bluer woman.
Someone asked her to smile & got mad once
the sun up & left room. *Sorry* she said
for I have conceived something
it will take the world
centuries to forget.

Haint Pink

What color is a haint's pussy? How do we know
she can't still cum? I had a friend who told a man
her pussy was his forever. I think he killed her.

He came to the funeral anyway. He wept like
he wanted the church to drown. At one point
he covered his ears, his face wretched like

God sent guilt. He spoke to me, & I tried
to turn my hate into one look. He wasn't
ever arrested, her case is still considered

open. Her case is gapped legged & tender,
& he walked out like he wasn't willing to see
what would float to the top. Like he couldn't stand
to hear his own name, like he would do anything

to make
all that
moaning
stop.

The Men Want to Know What Is Wrong

with me. They look me over & decide I must be a lemon.
My wiring is faulty, my exhaust thick & flooding the whole
neighborhood. I am certainly a problem. The men want to know

why I tried to have another woman do a man's job. They claim
they have no choice but to fix me. When they get up close, they see
nothing except bugs. Every bug has their face. Every face is

smashed

& blood scrap. Every scrap is fed to the wind. The men back off
slowly, like someone rewound how they approached me. I don't
say a word. I lick oil off my thumb, & I speed

the fuck off fast.

My windows are up. I unbury a song so loud, one
that no one can hear, beyond me. The men who see me pass them
by in the blur which I have settled in, they will wonder what song has
contorted my face like this, lugged the sweet water from my pores.
They honk. They curse. They will lie & say, *Your lights were too
bright* or *your gas tank was open.* They can help me. They can. They
can handle it if I just slow down & pull over. I will be
too busy making sure I can still
run good enough

to answer.

Chapter Five

Nothing But End Pieces of Bread

I have been in Sorrow's kitchen and licked out all the pots. Then I have stood on the peaky mountain wrapped in rainbows, with a harp and sword in my hands.
—Zora Neale Hurston, *Dust Tracks on a Road (1942)*

Urban Girl Exists

Somewhere between a rock & a God's place, at the intersection
of wanting to dye her hair into a slick sunset & wanting to
die, her hair: a slick sunset. Somewhere

between

Lake Erie & Atlantis, somewhere between yo boo & yo last
nerve. Somewhere wedged in food stamps & tramp stamps &
passport stamps. Somewhere between *people think*

I'm hilarious & I am probably just a joke.

                     In the center

of two steps forward & two steps back. Slipped
in betwixt a political campaign & a Black child being
peeled off a curb. Lodged within sociology reports & autopsy

reports, nestled between Beyoncé & the Block, linking the Hustle
& the Man, linking The Hustle & The Flow, linking The Boyz
& The Hood, linking The Menace & The Society. Somewhere tucked

within a razor blade & a roller dome. Central to
a cell block & a block party, between a cage & a mother's
nervous pecking, between addiction & affiliation. Right in

the midst of a gang sign & caution
tape. Between happy hour & the last call. In the seam of yo mama jokes
& her mama's screams. Amid yo sheets

& yo wallet, between a lover & a fist, between
a train & them tracks. Around the corner & around the coroner.

from edge & control, caught in the thick
of imperial avenue & heaven. Between forever
& never again.

Smack dab in the middle of death & defying.

Waste(full)

I wanted to feed my heart to the birds, but I heard if you feed a bird
the wrong thing it'll explode. What if my heart is the wrong thing?
What if my heart is a trick of the eye? The stripper's chainsaw grin?
The Xanax addict's plagiarized laugh? The booster's adrenaline
rush? What if my heart is
a Walkman someone broke in 8th grade? What if it is scratched
beyond recognition? & if I still have all the CDs for it? What if
some songs still play when you hit it against something sharp? What
if my heart is Renisha McBride's last knock? What if my heart's *help*
is answered in death?
What if my heart is the weed they claimed was in Sandra Bland's
system? What if my heart is Sandra Bland? What if
my heart no longer exists? What if my heart is Breonna Taylor
& they call my heart a criminal? What if my heart is Korryn Gaines
& my heart shoots back? & if my heart is
the crossroads Bone Thugs-N-Harmony crooned over? Would you
meet me there? Why did they take his Uncle Charles, y'all? What if
my heart is Uncle Charles, y'all? What if my heart is the projects?
What if everyone here is secretly trying to get out? What if the ones
who stay
are the ones they say ain't know no better? What if my heart is
Cleveland, Ohio, September 2015? What if my heart is 43 murders
in one month? What if my heart has 137 shots? What if my heart is
what a three-year-old boy named Major won't have but deserves?
What if my heart is a chance
to grow up? What if my heart is afraid to take chances? If it knows
those who might have lost them? What if my heart knows what it is
capable of & fears itself? What if my heart can't tell the difference
between humans & the birds? What if my heart knows the difference
but no longer cares?

How the Romans Must Have Treated Cleopatra in Egypt

You insist the girl lacks home training, but is she not a home?
Doesn't something live there? Why are you always here trying so
hard to prove it does not? *Barbaric,* you said? You do not say? Do
you know the etymology of the word? It's the Greek way to say
blabber, to say, *I don't know what you are saying because you are
foreign & offensive to my ears.* & so what if she never learned the
proper dinner party etiquette, why should she? She has always been
the dinner & the party, everyone has always assumed invitation. Bet
you came dressed to kill. Bet you can't pronounce the name of your
food. Obviously, you still finish it. Bet you say it is the cheapest thing
on the menu, bet it definitely tastes the best. You might describe it to
a friend as *a touch salty.* Tell 'em it had its sweet moments but

bitterness lingered in the finish. You bragged about the wine, then left
the bottle drained to jail dead flowers. You stole whatever shiny shit
you could get your heart on. You rinsed your hands in a dainty bowl
carved from war, left the spoils, waited for a thank you & then wiped
them on anything you considered worthless. You considered it all
worthless. You said you'd have a bill sent. You never paid. I doubt
you ever intended to. You demanded entertainment, then called every
single song obscene with lust in your jaw. You screamed debauchery,
then insisted on more. You asked why *all the art felt so angry.* It
dampened your mood considerably. You say something. You must
out of obligation. You have manners & truly you figure there is no
way to be a bad guest in a broken home. Who even cares enough to

notice a few missing items? Surely if not you, then someone else
would have. Why not smoke where there is already fire? Why not
leave the ruins trashed? What's another crime to a crime scene?

Atlantis, Discovered

I too told them the idea of so much clothing was absurd

I too told them my body was a power

a wedge of Africa they could never tame

You too look like Atlantis

the wand that chooses the hand that holds it

The girl who walks into the sea & swallows

her own

name.

Urban Girl Delicacies // 99 Cent Lip Gloss

being slick is damn near free. this is also how we learnt layers,
our first sticky situations, how we learnt what niggas want
us to taste like, even though it's impossible for us

to taste like an artificially made cherry. sometimes we stole it,

whole racks of man-made flavors. we'd hold the clear cylinders
& squeeze so hard the balls would pop out & a thick gush
would gather & eventually & without fail we would

ruin something we loved.

Hexes for My Exes

After Rachel Wiley, The Boss

Oh, ex-lover, I heard that you heard that
I no longer wish you shit. But that is not true—

I still wish you plenty of shit. For instance,
I wish you really, really good marijuana

then I wish you a marijuana tolerance so high
a session w/ Snoop Dog, Cheech & Chong, Wiz

Kalifa, Rihanna, Scooby & Shaggy + me will not
work. I wish you trips. I wish you plenty of trips.

I wish yo job stay tripping, I wish yo mom stay
tripping, I wish yo new boo stay tripping. I wish

every day of yo life was a fucking trip w/ truly
sensational weed that will not get you high. I wish

you into bars that serve everything except what
you want. I wish my heart to be the only thing on tap.

I wish you ring worms in your privates. I wish you
strap-ons that won't stay strapped on. I wish you scuffed

shoes after you buy them, for the first time, every time.
I wish you other loves, I do. I wish you loves

who claim they are nerds but don't know the difference
between Marvel & DC characters. I wish you loves who

tell you that they can't cook & they can. They just don't want to
cook for your punk ass. I wish you loves who tell you they can

squirt but it's really not squirt. I wish you end pieces of bread. I wish
you nothing but end pieces of bread. I wish you entire loaves

of end pieces of bread. I wish you into a world where chocolate does
not exist. A world where bloodthirsty ostriches roam the free land

searching for your blood. I wish you a world where there is no music
except Drake mixtapes. Which really ain't that bad. (Until it is)

all you got & then it's that fucking bad. I wish you
into a world where your tongue tastes everything as overcooked

okra, a world where my wishes were not so much like you: good
inside my mouth, meaningless the moment you left.

Tiffany Haddish as a Recipe for Joy During the Pandemic, & I Watched the Madam C.J. Walker Story & Found One Lie I Loved, Or

Brown Suga Da Secret

till it caramelizes into song. the song will be thick & sugary & burnt
& dripping & it will coat your throat like syrup. it is medicine, but you
can't tell the children that or they won't swallow. they gon' be dizzy,
become a bed of flower crowns, petal them asleep,

& if they wake with thorns, brew them into tea, steep them slow & let it
wake the others. allow the drinkers to decide if it is bitter or not. I know
women who are more lavender than anything else, pressed into

a book, a palm, a poem, a cure. I figure Eucalyptus had a short life
as a girl, quiet until she became useful, a balm on the tongue
of a woman. everything sweet ain't candy

& sometimes you just got to pick something up off the floor & put it in
your mouth & acknowledge God made it & it won't hurt.

Orange Is the New Blood

Orange became the old black.
The old black became the new
blood. The old blood became new

news—

Poussey is the first Black stud I see
on a television series as a main character.
She is well thought out, fairly complex,

& most importantly to my 9 a.m.
need to masturbate, she is fine af & eats pussy
in real life; so there is no suspension of disbelief

my orgasms must conquer in order
to complete themselves. I thank Netflix the moment
I meet her. The truth is I know she is going to die, I know why

she is visible. I know she is a point
they are trying to make; I know I can see myself
on television & I am supposed to say *thank you*. That's the point,

right? It's gasping for its very last
breath under a white man's weight but there it is,
shuddering. Do you know where a point goes when it dies? Do you

know there is no specific term to name the grief one feels
over a fictional character passing? When I was a kid,
I could not name what it meant

to watch G-Baby die in *Hardball,* or Thomas J. in *My Girl,*
or Mufasa in *Lion King,* or Ricky in *Boyz n the Hood.*
I wanted to but could not explain the loss of someone

I would never meet. How this too is a language where *stay* is
every word, & if such a thing is possible, there is
even less of a specific term

for when a fictional Black queer woman is murdered. The truth is
when Queen Latifa dies in *Set It Off,* I watch my first crush,
crushed in a very specific way. Urban lesbian disappears

to save her friends. I know she is going to die because she knows,
you can see it in her eyes when she raises her gun & fires
back, & the truth is by the time Snoop dies in *The Wire,*

I began thinking it'll be easier for me to plan
a funeral as opposed to a wedding. & the truth remains
it is even less of a specific term for saying goodbye to someone

introduced to you only so you can remember
what their corpse looks like. When Poussey dies,
the officer who kills her is painted as a victim; we are supposed to feel

sorry for the weight he is carrying underneath him. When Poussey dies,
we are supposed to remember her dimpled smile, we are supposed to see
Taystee rot in her own mouth—the show is about Piper,

after all; we all are reminded when it does indeed go on. When Poussey dies,
it ends unresolved because often so do we. When Poussey dies, we
are supposed to say *thank you.* We are to get on our knees

& thank the closest white God
that it wasn't Samira Wiley
this time.

Urban Girl Speaks to an Ex-Lover Out the Side of Her Neck Or Ode to The Maenad

& maybe i am where the wild things are & maybe you aren't thrilled

with the idea of your children growing inside the dark whispering

woods & maybe the noises i make at night remind you of a hunting

or a haunting & maybe you are afraid you will wake to me & find

a body you can't identify reeking of wine & blood & who needs

you?

Medium Rare

& what else is new? & what else is normal? & what else is rare?

& what else can I give to some(body)? & who are you to say *selfish*?

& can you say *drained*? & what can I expect in return? & will there
be enough for when I have children? & since it is inherited, what

will you expect from my children? & how will you get this blood
exactly? & what if you run out of needles? & will you move on

to knives? & will you move on to guns? & you aren't already

doing this? & you're absolutely sure about that? & you need me? &

you only need me in pints? & this won't kill me? & you are sure? &
I am saving (some) (one)? & how much blood did Koryn lose?

& did you send her some of mine? & why not? & I don't get to
decide where my blood goes? & if my guesses are all white

I am wrong? & you can't prove this by showing me? & I got this

blood from my father? & did you know he was murdered? & you

say this blood is so special? & why is it magik? & why could his own

magik not save him? & then who is the trick for? & who is clapping

& who is getting paid? & who goes home to their family feeling

better? & how many pints was that so far? & how many more

will you request? & do you really think you're sicker of my questions

than I am of your answers? Are you saving enough of my blood for

me? & what if something happens to me? & are you really calling me

selfish again? & if I give it to y'all, will y'all stop taking it?

& not just from me? & from Black bodies who don't offer it? & even

if they smoke weed & have rap sheets? & you promise me? & you

say I might feel faint once all of this is over & you say it might all be

over sooner than I expect? & why am I not surprised?

Urban Girl Is Her Own Nemesis
Or What to Do If

you want to run your well dry
& make the closest river a copy
cat, start refusing water slowly,

replace it with Pepsi & shots
of Hennessy. Hennessey is
a street that stumbled down

you & forgot who you were.
You're a street & every other lot
is empty. You think your brain is

the one with the baby dolls melting
into a thicket of grass. It's all limbs
& lace & sweetly painted neglect.

You want to grow weed in the back-
yard, so do it. You are going to get
caught, everything you do in the back

makes its way to the front. You know
that. You know enough to live & tell
about it. You can pretend that is enough

to survive. You can pretend to survive,
I've seen you slice open your own veins
& call it reign.

Chapter Six

Fortune of Bones

If I didn't define myself for myself, I would be crunched into other people's fantasies for me and eaten alive.

—Audre Lorde (1982)

You Are Never Too Young

to see a ghost. everyone knows that. kids even
see 'em easier, or so I've lived. Or so they've said,

or so you read in a small set of eyes in a neighbor
hood you only remember at 4:07 a.m. & you know

it's a thunderstorm somewhere with your heartbeat
& everyone is afraid to hear it but you. You run

to the windows & demand your pulse returned. You
race to the bed & dive under, ready to drag whatever

monster that is calling your name to the surface so it can
see the wild glint of its own celebrity in your too young,

too deathsharp eyes. You can't coddle it. You cannot do
what you don't know. You will try anyway. When it bends

the spoons, you will untwist them. Call it darling. Offer it
pudding. When the pudding weeps to the floor, you will slurp

it up. When the doors slam harshly, you will open them gently
with a smile. When the spirits anger & begin to wail & demand

to know why they are one endless ache & demand to know where
certain members of their families are, you will tell them the truth

as you know it. & when your mother demands to know
who on God's good green earth you are talking to? You will say

yourself & you will
have not told a single lie.

Haint Red

Someone made my jaw drop & I liked it enough to let them
do it again & again—until the ground beneath me wore hellish
lipstick in my shade. Someone rouged the streets with my face
resting in her palm, a pretty bug, but not too pretty not to squeeze
the flight from.

I ate Flamin' Hot Cheetos as a kid
no matter how bad it hurt the next day.
My mother is a nurse, she told me
what I was doing to my intestines, eating

the lining right out my stomach. I tried to be dainty
while licking my fingers & grinning like a girl already gone.

My older sisters say our dad comes back to them
as a robin. He only comes back to me as a nightmare
or a mirror, if there is any difference between the two

at all. I am both afraid of & scared for birds, it's hard

To explain & strange to feel. So I decide to make red
my favorite color. I eat apples & wait to discover something
good. I learn to cross my fingers, I decide to believe in luck.

In junior high my friends would use
cherry Kool-Aid to rinse their hair. I realized
my mama would whip my ass if I did what they did;
instead I offered to wash it from their scalps. I ain't mind
getting close to danger, I just knew better once than to bring it

home.

I sold poems in regular Swisher packets & called myself a hope
dealer. I blush a lot & people find that interesting on a Black
girl, so much so that they never consider the shame it takes to happen.

Humans have to crush something to create the color I have become.

Urban Girl & 100 Red Balloons

This has got to be *quick* & it was
so *this* should not be hard. That's what *they* tell you

to make *you* feel better. *They* is whoever *it* has not happened to,
it being whatever was

quick. My father gets shot in the head & dies
& I want you to think of 100 red balloons

being released at once. I want you to think of *this*
so you never have to think about what I think

about: *Where does a balloon go when popped?*
What land do you imagine for it if you could

never find every piece?

Hand-Me-Downs from the Dead, Or Replace *I* with *Joy*

A liquored goodnight at the end
of the floating man, my father is a ghost now
& I am halfblooded, I am a wound dragging itself

around the country. I only become festering if I just sit
here. A contagious rain sees me in its forecast. There I am,
a legacy of turbulence. A canon before it knows

it's supposed to explode, a borrowed burden
in the making. The first time I hear the word *lupus,* I am fastened
to a ceremony of mirrors. Too many are breaking for me to know

exactly how many
years of bad luck I am.

Fearless Sounds Like *Fatherless* on the Right Tongue

Orphan (n) Greek:
Orphanos: fatherless: literally deprived
Orbho: bereft from father

My father is in the audience & smiling & a ghost & this scares you.
Every time I write a poem about him, a bird flies out my chest, it flies
straight to the sun & it explodes before I can name it. All I got is this

featherless chest of wings. All I got is this fatherless fortune of bones.
All I got is a chest, but the treasure is for the drowned. The gold is
an ancient poison & it takes five seconds or five centuries, regardless,
it will take. If I drop a jewel & don't give you permission to pick it
up, then you have stolen water from the emptied well, then you have
demanded blood from the daughter of death, then you have

a merciless law, then you have a life spent in a spoilless war. Then you
see her tail. Then you see her teeth. Have you ever seen the siren's
father? He sits on a throne fashioned from skulls of non-believers.

His daughter is still learning how to swallow without shredding
her own throat. Do you know a legend when you be it?
If a human can't kill it, they name it a monster. If

a human can't own it, they call it impossible. His daughter
makes friends with the greedy gulls, their song tho
wretched & hungry is a familiar

salt. She loves the familiar, anything really
with family at the root. She doesn't pretend to be
beautiful. She doesn't pretend not to be either. Decked out

each spring, an old sword rusting
in her spine. Her father's pride in her
stance, every other sin belongs to her.
She walks a new plank, just a-whistling.

How Cleopatra Might've Felt in Cleveland, Ohio

Yo! Before we even get started, you ugly MFs ain't finna be mocking me
while I'm on this MF'ing stage. Like straight the f*ck up. —Bizzy Bone

When people only see you as a trend, it is extremely easy

for you to go out of style. When you are finally found
interesting, it is only after *urban* no longer means only
ghetto. Now that it's a brand, a runway, an advertising
campaign—you are all the rage. They been calling you

provocative, but now they mean it as a compliment.

Now you say *thank you* instead of *fuck you*. Now you learn

marketability. Now yo name looks good to a future employer.

It is quite cutting edge to have an "uncommon" name. Now it is

just a vibe to name your kids after things you love or things you

want. Or whatever you find beautiful. You have no time to

wonder what or who has been fed off your sorrow. They claim

they too are self-made, meanwhile, they get to count coattails

instead of coins & carnage. Today the whites will twerk with

you. They will yell, *Go off.* Other Black people

will remind them that they aren't your kind of Black that
they are better off, refined & will only return to the hood
in rap songs. They will refuse to make eye contact with you
in public. They will put you on then take you off, at leisure.

Today you belong

to the masses, for thirty seconds you are a commercial. 15

minutes of blame. Centered. Staged. Consumerism. Keeping

you alive & killing you. Today you survive & people point

at you like a many-eyed creature whose pain may help

someone else learn

not to be a bad person. Tomorrow

you will tell them, how you knew

the whole time, that all your blood

was their favorite part.

Urban Girl Writes Her City's Name on Tomorrow
For Cleveland, Ohio

I do not blame the dirt
for wanting to shimmer.
I blame the water for thinking
it's too good to make mud.

1.
Some people think my city is a punchline.
They think we're really bad at sports & staying
alive. That we're so ugly no one would ever
put a ring on it.

Why do birds fly backwards over Cleveland?
——'Cause there is nothing worth shitting on!

What's the difference between Cleveland & a bucket of shit?
——The bucket!

Some people think we have the filthiest
mutherfucking mouths in the Midwest.
My city thinks some people are what happens
when you don't grow up here, when you grow up sure

tomorrow knows your name & calls it
till you answer. My city thinks that's a joke it will only get
in hindsight. My city don't get nothing till after the fact, till Lebron
returns, till the protesters leave, till the crime rates drop some.

My city might not be here when that happens, might be
at the crossroads waiting for everyone else.
                              ——Who's there?
                    ——Cleveland.

——Lock the doors & turn off the lights!

My city makes the apocalypse look reasonable
to outsiders. My city looks itself in the face every morning
without wincing. My city can't say its own name without hearing
Tamir Rice scream, without hearing no scream at all

from three-year-old Major. My city is a dead baby joke you snickered
at & are embarrassed about.   *How do kids from*
Cleveland spend their first week of school?
                              ——Studying
——their Miranda rights!

2.
Cuyahoga County was named by the Seneca Native
Americans. It means "place of the jawbone." The jawbone is
the hardest bone to break & typically is the first place punched.
I did not read this anywhere. My father told me when I was eight.

He said no one alive knows what or who, but our city was struck in
the jaw. He says when the Cuyahoga River caught flames, it was
blood stepping outside getting some fresh air. He said it was all
of our blood, anyone who was ever born or will ever be born

in Cleveland, & they think our blood is dirty &
they think we're all wounds festering, & they think we will
infect them, & sometimes no one even notices a person's problems
until they set themselves on fire. My city is a proud pyromaniac

licking ashes off its fingers. My city knows the recipe for making
water thicker than blood. My city would tell you,
but it does not trust you
not to laugh.

We Are Torn

old stamps licked in the same wound
daily, stuck to each other. I will remember
where I was when they killed Trayvon Martin.

Ann Coulter says her Blacks
are better than our Blacks. Exactly how
many Blacks you got over there, Ann?

I will remember where I was when they killed
Trayvon Martin. A congested swamp of Florida
bones settled in my chest. Exactly how many Blacks

you got over there, Ann? Are they all still
alive? A congested swamp of Florida bones settled
in my chest. I pray my one-day son won't be one

of your Blacks. Are any still
alive? Do your Blacks make it, Ann? I pray
my one-day son won't be one of your Blacks.

Do you only collect the living or do you
also hoard the dead? Do your Blacks make it,
Ann? My one-day son asks for candy, shall he

be chastised in cavities or bullets? Do you
only collect the living or do you
also hoard the dead? In what manner

do you mark your belongings?
My one-day son asks for candy, shall he be
chastised in cavities or bullets? How many times a year

do your Blacks visit the mortician? In what manner
do you mark your belongings? The prideless beg
of blood? How many times

a year do your Blacks visit the mortician?
Is that covered under your insurance? The pride
less beg of blood? Was Mike, Tamir, Eric,

Freddie, or Jordan any of your Blacks?
Well the police gave 'em to God. Is that covered
under your insurance? When you grow

out of your Blacks,
where do you plan
to hide the bodies?

Urban Boy Lives

For Marshawn McCarrel

I hope you still living
Somewhere the explosion is a sunrise

worth racing towards. Between being
the reason for the protest
& leading it. Somewhere
God's cry & your mother's cry don't mix.

Somewhere the blunts be

as endless as you are. Somewhere in a rap lyric
everyone thinks they know the words to but stumbles over
then forgets & then looks up one day & can't find it anywhere.
but still hums with all their heart,

Somewhere everything is

a healing. You blink & your dreams come
true. You un-cry & un-scab & un-shatter. Your very bones are
butterflies—I am sorry this world is full of nets. Your sweet skin
is a wolf's howl, every kiss feels like the moon.
Your entire voice is a sky.

Somewhere between
how you died & why

The Such Thing as the Stupid Question

Where are you from???
When I say *ancestors,* let's be clear:
I mean slaves. I'm talkin' Tennessee
cotton & Louisiana suga. I mean grave

dirt. I come from homes & marriages
named after the same type of weapon—
all it takes is a shotgun to know

I'm Black. I don't got no secrets
a bullet ain't told. Danger see me
& sit down somewhere.

I'm a direct descendant of last words
& first punches. I got stolen blood.
My complexion is America's

darkest hour. You can trace my great
great great great great grandmother back
to a scream. I bet somewhere it's a haint

with my eyes. My last name is a protest;
a brick through a window in a house
my bones built. One million

scabs from one scar.
Heavy is the hand that held
the whip. Black is the back that carried this

country & when this country's palm gets
an itch, I become money. You give this country
an inch & it will take a freedom. You can't talk slick

to this legacy of oiled scalps. You can't spit
on my race & call it reign. I sound like my mama now,
who sound like her mama who sound like her mama who

sound like her mama, who sound like her
mama who sound like her mama who sound like her
mama who sound like her mama, who sound like a scream.

& that's why I'm so loud, remember? You wanna know
where I'm from? Easy. Open a wound
& watch it heal.

A Lineage of Language

Got eyes in da back of my head *begat* every shuteye
ain't sleep *begat* everything you do in the dark will come

out in the light *begat* stay out the kitchen if you can't stand
da heat *begat* a watched pot won't boil *begat* a pot calling

the kettle Black *begat* tha blacker tha berry/ tha sweeter
da juice *begat* beauty is only skin

deep but ugly is to the bone *begat* can't see the forest
for tha trees *begat* between a rock & a hard place *begat* blood

is thicker than water *begat* not a pot to piss in or a window
to throw it out of *begat* a wet pussy & a dry purse don't match

begat a hard head make a soft behind *begat* don't write a check
yo ass can't cash *begat* a hit dog will holler *begat* I brought you

in this world & I will take you out *begat* don't
let your right hand know what your left hand is doing *begat* step

on a crack break yo mama's back *begat* do as I say
not as I do *begat* don't bite

off more than you can chew *begat* don't bite tha hand dat feed you
begat God made dirt, dirt don't hurt put it in yo mouth

& make it work *begat* eaten out of house & home *begat* stay in
a child's place *begat* smelling yo self *begat* you smell like outside *begat*

stop running in & out my house *begat* hush *begat* enough
is enough *begat* I'm not the one *begat* I am not one

of your lil friends *begat* I'm not so & so's mama *begat* fix
yo face *begat* stop all that crying befo' I give you sumtin'

to cry about *begat* do I look
like "Boo Boo the Fool" *begat* do YOU got McDonald's money

begat cash rules everything around me *begat* come hell
or highwate*r begat* do or die *begat* go for broke *begat* you will

catch more flies with honey than with vinegar *begat* money over bitches
begat bitch please *begat* Black is beautiful *begat* a day late

& a dollar short *begat* talk to the hand *begat* you go girl *begat* sikkke
begat all that & a bag of chips *begat* open

a can of whip ass *begat* check yo tone *begat* watch yo mouth *begat* WAP
begat respectfully stay out

my mouth.

I was a match made in heaven /when hell was a pile of wood /
I run through hell, / with gasoline drawers on / Stop to tell the devil /
that God is good. —Lil Wayne

You Don't Tell Other Niggas in the Hood You Are Creole

Cus, you are still a nigga, ok? They gon' tell

you. You ain't nothing

but a nigga. Understand that shit.

Look in the mirror & say, *I'm a nigga.*

If the mirror is broken, then it's 14 years of bad luck 'cause

you a nigga. Nigga.

& niggas got to do twice as much

as everybody else. Nigga listen to me, they don't care

what language you speak. So what? It's nigga

with gumbo. Alligator-eating ass nigga. Swamp Nigga

Eve's Ba-you-Felicia ass nigga. Ain't nobody trying to hear

a nigga speak French.

My cousin wanted to warn me before

I opened my mouth & showed off a target. Don't even

say "Louisiana" until you can spell

it. If they ask about the chicken bones, you lie

& say "BBQ." If they want to know if you know voodoo,

say anything but Great Grandma's maiden name.

That night I scrubbed myself

a new tongue. Bathtub broiled me crawfish

red while I listened to Lil' Wayne for the first time

& I swear he sounded

just like home

after a robbery.

Chapter Seven

What Starts Wail Ends Well

1,2,3 The devil's after me, 4-5-6 he's always throwing sticks, 7-8-9 he misses every time, Hallelujah, Hallelujah, Hallelujah, Amen.
—As heard through the ears of Ladybug in *Crooklyn (1994)*

I Met Urbanshee & She Gave Me a Name

Of course I can't tell you
my name, you will use it

like it's yours. You might sell it
for an enchanted hand

full of knuckles & praise. You might
use it against me. A march of grinning ghosts

know how to spell my name so it reads
as a warning. A child outside of my corner store carries

two razors in the soft beds of her
jaws; she plants them in whatever tries to ruin her.

This is a hint. Here is another: a starved dog
on the blvd is a monster. She has worked hard to be.

A stern grooming, firm betrayals & trained by fear,
what has being man's best friend done

for anyone? Her claws? My name spelled
backwards & forwards, my name means replenished

blood. My name only dances naked in mirrors or cemeteries
& only when it can't tell the difference. My name is the backdrop

for a haunted portrait. The portrait is of a princess or a sacrifice
or a poison. Or all three neatly tucked into one another.

Started from the Bottom Now I'm Sula

Folks were demanding my head & I felt kind, enough
to indulge them with one finger. I died once trying
to do things their way. I got so worried I was gon'

end up alone & then it happened anyway so now
I don't fear any quiet unless it comes from me or God.
Old friends gave me the silent treatment & I said *thank you.*

I can hear myself think & it sounds like a haint escaped.
It's hard to trust a creature you can't name, so they named me
cruelly out of love, I think. My name is a fossil,

an apple & a snake married in thick rich amber. I skint the apple
& ate it. I skint the snake & I ate it too. Ohio was nothing but water
once, my name means that. Or the glacier mid-thaw. Or just a strange
place where life still lives in the frozen. Ya know
some folks go straight to hell & some folks have had practice
& some folks have had to dig their way up to find any

paradise. I know of an island that disappears
on principle. It does not get into long explanations on why or even
how it does this. It just does. That is my name in the witch's book,

an island in a lake. My lake is Erie too. Birth marked
& mocked. The fairies are all copper & their breath smells
like paper cuts. Everyone's best friends here until they aren't.

There are a few ways to form a lake island; one way is erosion.
The separation where breaking is important. Humans always play
a significant role. Naturally occurring

disasters do their part   but the *truest* way to form
a lake island is through the buildup of sedimentation. When
you chip something hard, it does not become less hard,

just smaller. Odd, isn't it? How hailing means to praise
& also means the atmosphere has created something sharp.
Perhaps all the tiny shards collect & every fracture forms a fault.

& perhaps all the faults collect & every fault forms a woman
surrounded by shore. Quick, if a deserted island is trapped, what
would bring you? A rogue storm? An incredible risk. A dream wild

with its own theories? That was a trick question. The real
question is *once you get there, is it still considered deserted?*
When we die, most of us will not die saints, but for a second

let's imagine. What would it hurt anyway? Me, I am Saint of Salt
Tossed Behind a Shoulder. Saint of the Sucked Teeth. Saint of Sulas,
I bled my way back to myself, left crumbs of myself to remember

Where I came from. I pulled a purpose out of thin air.
Every knife I have ever owned once lived in my back.
I taught myself how to kiss myself & then did it over & over.

I fed folks with nothing but what I was left with.
When I got hungry, I ate the very ground
I walked on. I saw so many I love killed

& still managed to bring some life back
into my eyes. So I ain't perform many miracles.
But let me tell you this:

Once
when everyone I knew was watching,
I turned a child's tears into a worthwhile adult.

It Is Hard to Tell Someone On Fire That You Are Drowning

They will be jealous of the water. Still. Even as it rises to your nose.
My mother explains this calmly, like there aren't bubbles coming
out of her mouth, like the shark ain't

belly up & floating at the top, like I never noticed what our home is
since my father was killed. Had she always been an aquarium?
A box of water, temperature regulated,

organisms inside growing & needing, had she always been
accustomed to being stared at, how many fingerprints has she
never come clean of? If

one? My mother is her most kind when she is quiet. Sacrifice is
not a shattering of glass, it is blood on your hands for getting
someone out alive. My mother

clouds when she don't want nobody to see her pain, which is how
I inherited my blur. Our shark is dead, but she does not want us to see
it *this way.* The fin is mostly gone,

the eyes look less dead when they are facing her. My mother, she is
her most gentle when there is no other choice.

What Starts Well Ends Wail

Urbanshee gave birth to a New Dark

& maybe God sent an angel to explain what was going on

& Urbanshee said Fuck that or maybe Urbanshee sent God an angel

to explain & God said Oh me, oh my child you deserve rest. &

Urbanshee's thighs opened into storm clouds & the rain

tasted like a few winter sunsets, purples, pinks, reds, & frost.

The New Dark crept out quiet as dew & the umbilical cord was

a burning bridge & when the last of it was ash, every bird in the

world lost a feather & Urbanshee felt plucked into recognition.

& the New Dark looked at Urbanshee & neither wept. Legend has it,

you can hear them, cackling still, wind slurping through sky.

Urbanshee held the New Dark up to both breasts until we had a milked

river. Nothing screamed that evening. No wise men showed up but

Urbanshee ain't know man anyhow. Three wise women appeared

just to make a point. The tobacco witch, a seven tongued whore, &

a storyteller in her third century, all of them kin through one curse or

another. Gifts were given to the New Dark, cans of haint skin &

400 acres of to be continued from the storyteller. The whore gave

one of her tongues, her sharpest tooth, & then snuck the address

of a lady who can change everything, into the New Dark's nose.

The tobacco witch went last, her & Black Mary had been smoking &

pissing in an enemy's rose bush or so that tale went, but once they was ready, they spit themselves into the New Dark's parched ears. Urbanshee grinned & burned a country's worth of plantations, then buried Urbanshee's placenta in its place. Urbanshee decided to name the New Dark after this very act & God looked down & said *Fine*.

Another Poem about My Dead Father

My father is dead.

I notice it most during things
that haven't happened yet:

My father is dead at my wedding.
He is a slow dance of bullets,
an autopsy trying

to make polite conversation
with the guests. My flower girl
is me at every age

he did not see me turn.
I am throwing things
I haven't seen in years:

> my virginity, pigtails,
>> my diploma, joy,
>>> & names
>>>> of old lovers.

My father is dead at the birth
of my first child. The doctor asks,
Where is the father?

I say *murdered* out of habit.
The doctor does not specify,
so neither do I.

Instead we both stare
at my child who is named
after the chill in the room.

My father is dead
at my death bed. We play
Blackjack until the light comes.

When it does, he lifts me
onto his shoulders. I get the piggyback ride
promised to a child who time has been waiting on.

I Would Be So Sad If I Fucked Up & My Father Came Back as a Zombie

Which is something
I have to remember
when I pray for his return.
My mother says *be careful*
what you wish for & to be honest
I'm not really a careful bitch on
average, when it comes to wishing,
I'm even worse. I kinda assume
the universe knows what I mean
even when I don't—so in case
I have fucked up thoroughly,
which according to the law of me,
is always a possibility, I want to be
perfectly clear in stating I want him back,
yes certainly, without a doubt. But not
like that. Not with his brain stuck blooming
like strange roses. Not a husk where the whole
once was, not someone asking me to kill him,
again. I've been preparing for a zombie apocalypse
in small ways since I was 16, since my dad's blood
smeared my childhood, his murder: an announcement
that shit can & will get real. Dystopian & Fantasy novels
taught me adaptation is just one long magic trick. I have
books I believe in more than most people. As a kid, I read
R. L. Stine's "ChooseYour Own Adventure.' I would choose
wrong the first time, all the time. My daddy would find me,
furiously flipping pages, holding back tears, eyes big like
his, trying desperately to find my mistake, he'd ask me
to stop, he'd say *Babyo, you scaring us both*
you got to let it go & even then I found it
so hard to accept without a fight.

Haint Glitter

What do you call a girl
who has been haunted more years

than she has not? Her father was murdered.
If you kill her, he'll die twice. You can't
charge someone for the same crime

in America, she is triple jeopardy. Do you know
how hard it is to protect a ghost? Do you know how
hard it is for a ghost to protect a girl?

It's like grasping glitter with an invisible pair
of tweezers. The ghost, the father, he is neither
here nor there & the girl, she is both.

What is *protection* but a breath shared or given
willingly? What is *willingly* but a gift
with no receipts?

What is a *receipt* but a catalog of what you got
& what you paid & what you owed flashing
before your eyes

& what is this but being *Black*
in every life
you choose to live?

7 Lessons That Blood Taught Me

someone can put all of you in a bag & carry you away
some people will say you won't even feel the pain
but for a moment

being thicker than water means nothing if you aren't sure
you won't eventually dissolve into it.

getting left on the curb does not make you a bad person. a stain is
only something that will never go away completely

recognize a leach, sooner than liters

if you are going to spill pray
something is there to catch you

being blue inside makes it easy for everyone else
to see you as red when you come out, a thick clot
iron clad & running

everything I was born with
came with a price

What Is C.R.E.A.M.?

What is a '90s song by Wu-Tang Clan? What is a group decision
made from desperation? What is a breathless block? What are hearts
gone gold? What was one of my father's favorite songs?

What is the Midas wrist? What's a summer without fresh blood?
What is generational trauma tipping a scale in a dirty basement?
What is my business all in the streets? What is my childhood in a pop

culture reference? What is
a damned shame? What is a shame
—damned?

Pop Quiz: Do You Understand What You Are Reading?

1. Define irony
   E.g.: my heart is a Band-Aid for other hearts that have been bloodied
   by other hearts & once they heal, they rip me away. I am sullied
   with a healing not my own. What is iron(y):

   a. How blood turns brown
   b. How brown turns blood
   c. All of the above

2. Around here bullets do have names & you need to know
   every single one *by heart, by skull, by the way the mother screams bloody
   murder.* How do you name your brown child?

   a. Name your brown child something that will look good on a job
      application
   b. Name your brown child something that will look good on a T-shirt
   c. Name your brown child something that will look good on a tombstone
   d. Name your brown child something that will look good to God

3. The speed of brown death is?

   a. An uncontrolled variable
   b. A controlled variable
   c. The public is still deciding if it matters or not

4. How do you measure brown grief?

5. How many answers were erased just because
   you thought they were wrong?

6. Please use this space to draw anything you like
   except a gun:

When I First Saw a Haint, Or Cleopatra Came Back

For Seconds, I did not scream. It did. I knew it

wanted to suffocate me. My own piss at this point

knew better than to come uncalled. Ancestral rage

inherit & limitless, I was six & more than a few lives

before this. Two freckles on my inner wrist, puncturing

a river of caramel. No fear of snakes. An affinity for libraries

& gold. My grandfather would say *baby you something else.*

I never had to ask what. It was not the only one to come back

with a different ending in mind.

Urban Girl Delicacies // Revenge

When my feet feel like four miles of my own decision making,
I smile the stripper's smile, I blink blank & lust the tiger out,
her stripes are black as mine, you inch in, think you want to see
her teeth, until you see past them, the gallows hanging there
pink & swaying. The cave in which they hang, lit only by fire,
& you can't see who started it. It smells sweet & archaic—
like a grave filled with love letters. Any further & you will fall
into the pit. Any further & you will look down, you will see all
the bodies & wonder how they got there. You won't believe
they are real. You won't believe I am real either. What else but
magic could convince a human it won't bite?

First of All

The day I was born I saw my granddaughter.
She has a tattoo of a face that is mine boasting
down her wicker basket of a back. She is naked
from the waist up dancing in a quicksand of lovers.

The tattoo looks nothing like me *now*. The eyes are too sure.
The smile is not sure enough. One day there will be no differences.
Whatever years I have left will be spent becoming the woman who
turns her daughter's daughter's back into a mosaic memory. This

morning I become a countdown that ends with me becoming
a portrait aging in a museum of all my best choices. The day I was
born, a banshee spoke for the first time in a long time, she said, *You
will send them all to us with their heads still on.* She told the sirens

to tell me, *You are a language ready to be learned. A nest
of folklore that has gathered itself for the girl children. A pirate ship:
the crew, the jewels, the dead things. The sea air bloated with its own
salt. The hot laughing rum; the walking of the plank. Anchors made*

from shark teeth & mirrors. The day I was born someone was
murdered & then someone else & then someone else & then someone
else & then someone else & then someone else until it was my father
& then I lost count. The day I was born my mother woke

Urbanshee & Urbanshee winked an answer only the enchanted know.

Acknowledgements

For God & all your grace & mercy, for love & all its capacity. **For My DaddyO, Gregory Rodgers**, I've been writing this book since the moment you were murdered, i gave this book the same amount of years i had with you. I know you in heaven handing out copies. You gifted me boundless joy, audacity & imagination. When this world felt too small you taught me to believe in bigger ones. I wanted more than Cleveland to know your name, more than me to feel your impact & everyone to see our endless & unwavering love. Time is still on our side——afterwhile crocodile. **For My MommyO, Tracy Freeman**, you are the original badmamajamma. The reason endurance dances in my bones. You have held me up in my worst moments & held me down until we got to better moments. There is no world where you are not my hero. This book is a testament to your resilience, it was so much it couldn't just live in your body but migrated to mine, thank you for this inheritance of hope, this legacy of loving-regardless. **For My Big Sisters NikkiMama (nikkimama, nikkimama like dat) & AngieO**, the best gift i have ever gotten was having you two as big sisters. Mommy really showed out. I would choose you both again in every life. We 3 the hard way. 3 the cool way. The power of three, the Charmed sisters aint got shit on us .me & yall—us never part./aint no mountain aint no sea/ take my sisters away from me/ da-di-da-da/ **For Wendy Freeman,** my bonus big sister, I'm glad Angie chose you, and you chose all of us back. **For my Grandparents Andrew & Rachel Freeman**, it was the family trips down south, it was you two telling me stories of family, of blackness, of magic & laughter & sorrow & hope that made me want to be a writer. It was you who took me to theater & slam practice. It was you who pinned money in my bra for greyhound trips. I can never repay you & you never once asked. I love you. **For My Granny Majorie Johnson**: every birthday, every xmas, every holiday or weekday that you got me books, you got me new friends, each helped me get here. **For MY FIANCE S.J**—lol, this is my first official announcement to the world. You, my love are so much of the reason this book got completed, you sat through tantrums & endless blk n mild smoke, you celebrated the triumphs when i did not have the energy to, when darkness came you did not sit with me in the dark, you gathered bouquets of light until i had enough seeds to grow more. You are a happily ever after. I knew you were coming the whole time. **For My Future Mother In Love Denise**, thank you for SJ, b ut also for you, you are a bonus mom in all the best ways. **For my whole entire family, both living & dead: The Freemans (like the boondocks or lovecraft country) The Rodgers, The Atkins, The Marks, The Goss's,** Yall are & will always be everything to me. Its too many of us to name & yall will claim im acting funny if i dont name em all, lol, just know my love for you is endless!!!!! **For my best friend Tiffany Harris**: growing up & Urban girl with you, has been nothing less than an honor. There is nothing we haven't survived together. There is nothing we cant survive together. You are a blessing Tippy. **For the cousins I grew up with Drew, Quest, Jazzmin, Marie, Dirt, Keon, Lil Marcus, Lil Micheal, & Aziza**, you made childhood & adulthood equally enjoyable, bebe's kids, the lot of us. For **My Nieces & Nephews Sho-Sho, Makari, Miles, Sho-Sho Jr, Bella, Amare', Nzari, Bella, Radia, Drew 4th, Piper, Holden, Clem, LuLu**, y'all are some of the best people i have ever loved, i'd do anything for you (Jay Z song plays immediately). **For My Coven Rachel Wiley & Rachel Mckibbens**: our bond is one that i hold close & fiercely, i was a little sister as a gift already & to be a little sister again as a choice is gift upon gift.Your hearts howl is my hearts howl, always. **For My Lil sisters, Blythe Baird, Isis Duncan & B.G & My Lil Bro Papi**, each of you are a wish granted. I would grow new teeth to protect you. I would volunteer as tribute every time. **For My Gibby Gibb Gibbs,** your love is a compass to adventure & a lighthouse back home, my friend i wouldn't have finished this book without you & your insistent & gentle nudging, without your sweet patience and endless tenderness, you helped me through & through & through and thank you for reintroducing me to **Megan Falley**, thank you for caring about my work and for reminding me that I believe in 2nd chances. **For my bbymama Jzl Jmz:** Thank you for helping me name so much of what I thought was unnameable, including this book. You are both effortlessly brilliant & effortlessly hot. **For Nina Domingue-Glover, Stephanie Fields & Zuggie Tate,** you were here for this book in its infancy, you sat with each of these stories & me until we felt in place"She is a friend of my mind. She gather me, man. The pieces I am, she gather them & give them back to me in all the right order. It's good, you know, when you got a woman who is a friend of your mind." **For My Oak Hall 200: Tor'e, Tiffany, Shayna Marie, Lexx & (sometimes) Shay**, because yall are who i would set it off wit **Pink Door Fellows**, May we all be forever feral in our joy. **For The Watering Hole & Specific shout out to my cohort noor ibn najam, Angelo Geter, Daniella Tossie-Watson, Micheal Frasier, Junious Ward, & Our coach Tyhiemba Jess**: It was an honor to read your brillant work & have your generous eyes on my own. You all truly to be a better reader & writer. **For The WinterTangerine Manuscript Cohort, kiki nicole, Golden, Yujane Chen & Lyrik Courtney, & My mentor Yasmin Belkhyr** for helping me believe a manuscript was possible. **For any & everyone who participated in the 2021 Black Joy Experience**: we are the future & nothing but the future my loves. **Team Yellow Brick Road Vitamin Cea, Divine Raynell, My Oliv Branch, Brittany Carter, Catrina Brenae, Dequadray "D.W" White, MarXus Rhodes, DiJa, & zak**, yall are the very picture of chosen family in the dictionary of my life. Yall all look good as hell in the picture. Yall are courage & brain & heart & a home worth returning to. **For Lou Barret** my virgo force & partnering with me to make great things, like Outsiders Queer Midwest Retreat, speaking off i forever love all the participants <3. **For Mrs. Watkins-Clark, Mrs. Sorrells, Damien Nova, Ray Gorgano, Ms. Gorman, Liberty, Will Evans, Izetta Nicole, Scott Woods, Tom Noy, Thomas Budday, J.G., Billy Tuggle, Karen akak Fairy Godmommy, Auntie Antoinette, Native Child & Soup, Peace & JBell, Anthony Amptified Evans, T Miller, Tia Christina, Tira "Free" Heard, Joseph Harris, Angelique Palmer, Sarah Myles Spencer, Su Flatt, One Truth, Jess & Sian Wright**, you have been hands & hearts on my work, my personhood or both, either way i am better for it & absolutely grateful. **For Jonathan Lykes, Shameeka Moore, Tomisha Harper, Durand Benard, Infinity Coleman, Joshua "Scribe" Watkis, Malachai & Bri Maisha, Clarity Levine, Elle Belle, Redd, Emia Jae, Barbra Fant, Chris Webb, Kalim, Tim Luttermoser, Tyler, Timothy DuWhite, Raja Freeman, Sha'condria "Icon" Sibley, Princess, Erich Slikmak, Ephriam, Abigail Carney,**

KK, Marcel & Nika Price, Marzai Sadler, Mia Monet, Damien, Venus Di' Khadija Selenite, Zach Hannah, G Foster, KFG, Allison Kennedy, D'eja' Kahlo, Jon Jon Moore, & My good Taurus sis Jocelyn Nemiah Spencer, Keisha Soleil & QueenLacheifa, Lucas Grover, Traci Haze, Dylan Butler, Ashly Jade, & the homies with Underdog Academy For growing up with me & my art & allowing me to do the same with you & yours (summa of since BNV days) For Ebony Stewart, Toni Morrison, Natasha Oladokun, Octavia Butler, April Sinclair, Audre Lorde, Aiera D. Matthews, Ali Black, Zora Neale Huston, Airka Foreman, Angela Davis, Assatta Shakur, Virginia Hamilton, Porsha O., Chauvet Bishop, April Ranger, Gala Mukomlova, Nyuma Waggeh, Omer A, Jeananne Verlee, Faylita Hicks, Sierra DeMulder, Tank, Oz. Longworth, Lil Wayne, Tracy Chapman, Dr. Tara Betts, Domonique C, Dave Lucas, Every member of Bone-Thugs-N-armony, Khalisa Rae, Mo Browne, Grace Akon, Seph Young, Giddy Perez, Danez Smith, Simone Pearson & so many many more your art has opened the doors for my art, in so many ways, some of you i may never say thank you to personally, & some i have & dont mind saying it again, to you all:here are your flowers. Tanesha Tyler, THIS WOULD HAVE BEEN IMPOSSIBLE WITHOUT YOU CUZ, you legit made this process which was quite scary to me, delightful & educational, you made me feel seen, heard & cared for the entire time. I wish a spirit like yours to every author & their first endeavor towards the publishing world, you are gem of gems. Ruth Awad, what a dream of an editor you are!!! You were attentive to each word, each concept, each story. You, fellow world builder, helped me establish the rules for this one & you my dear are welcome anytime. For Kalise & Joplin & Storytime For Hanif Abdurraqib, i first sent this manuscript to you at Button uncertain, you helped me become concrete in that purpose. For Sam, for all those chit chats after slams, to you making space for my first book, thank you my g, sincerely. For the entire Button team & Roster. For WestSide Community House, all my coworkers, & all my past & present students—with all my love to my squad jr aka my students from summerofsisterhood 2021 & the teaching artist Coach Pinque, Mrs. Bri, Mr John, Ms Day & Ms. Maia. Yall made me realize this book could be in beautiful

hands. For First Zion Missionary Baptist Church, Pastor Charles who baptized me, all the sisters, deacons, deaconess, nurses, mothers & family, you nourished my very soul. For Playhouse Square & Brave New Voices for helping me meet my first love, poetry. For Cleveland Public Theater & all my coworkers, yall reminded me of ALL the ways I could write & bring life to my art. For Karamu Theater, for being here in Cleveland & Black this long. Thank you For Center For Arts Inspired Learning & all my coworkers & past & present students, for teaching me how much i love being a teacher. For St. Clair & Superior & Cleveland & Ohio For The 2008 Charles F Brush graduating class of 2008. For my sweet cavapoo Doobie Doodle Doo your fur-cuddles & nips of encouragement did the actual work. For everyone & everywhere Urban. Rip, Daddy, Jessica Coleman, Marshawn McCarrel, Lauren Block, Giselle "auntie G" Robison, Nanny, Jewel N, Aunt Rose & Aunt KAT, Godfather Gat, Rage, Aunt Penny, Nika Price, & to all the ancestors who speak up for me & speak through me, your guidance is unmatched.

This space is for people who are no longer in my life but helped form the woman who wrote this book

_____

If i forgot someone, know that i am incredibly sorry & love you so much & this space is for you & your glorious name

_____

Notes

The quotes from Chapter One, Once Upon a Time on Loop, "**Lida 'Stony' Newsom:** *Ya'll niggas done lost ya'll mind. We might as well not even talk about this shit no more.* & **Francesca 'Frankie' Sutton:** *Well I'm talkin' 'bout it. And ain't nobody gon stop me from talkin bout it.*" Are from *Set It Off (1996)* one of the authors top 5 favorite movies.

"On Glorification" first appeared in *BOAAT* (March/April, 2018).

"X Things They Never Tell You about the Drug Dealer's Daughter" first appeared online via Button Poetry (2014), & was first said aloud on a Father's Day, during a slam meeting.

"The Author Explains Necromancy" first appeared in *The Offing* (2019) as "When I Speak of Hunger" & was written in a Winter Tangerine Workshop, from a prompt by Jayy Dodd.

"I Wonder What Happens to the Black Little Girl from *Kill Bill Vol. 2*" was based in lore from the movie *Kill Bill Vol. 2* (2004), written & directed by Quentin Tarantino. The character being discussed in the poem, Nikki, is played by actress Ambrosia Kelley & is the daughter of the character Copperhead, played by actress Vivica A. Foxx.

"Urban Girl in Four Non-Oscar-Nominated Parts," parts 1, 2, 3, & 4 are all based in lore from *Set It Off* (1996), directed by F. Gary Gray and written by Kate Lanier and Takashi Bufford. Parts 1, 2, & 3 present the characters in the order they died. Part 1's focus is the character Tisean "T.T" Williams, played by actress Kimberly Elise. Part 2's focus is the character Cleopatra "Cleo" Sims, played by actress Queen Latifia, & her girlfriend, Ursula, played by actress Samantha McLachlan; the poem also ends with a reference to Shug & Celie, two characters in the novel/movie *The Color Purple*. Part 3's focus is the character Francesca "Frankie" Sutton, played by actress Vivica A. Foxx and the title is her exact quote from the movie. Part 4's focus is Lida "Stoney" Newsom, played by actress Jada Pinkett Smith.

The quote from Chapter Two, Ancient like Darkness, is from the movie *Eve's Bayou* (1997) written & directed by Kasi Lemmons. The Witch is played by actress Diahann Carroll & Aunt Mozzelle is played by actress Debbi Morgan. This film is another movie in the author's top 5, and the author is one degree of separation from this movie, as someone she knows & loves dearly appears both in the film & the author's acknowledgements.

"The (Urban) Urban Legend" first appeared in milkjournal.net (2017).

"No Tradebacksies" first appeared in *Freezeray Poetry* (2017).

"Urban Girl Finally Responds to the Yo Mama Jokes" first appeared in *Theories of Her* anthology from Mercurial Noodle press (2016) & then again online via Button Poetry (2017).

"Haint Green" first appeared in *Josephine Quarterly* (2020).

Suga On The Flo was released by Etta James in 1978 & has become a piece of my living body.

"How Cleopatra Must Have Felt in Rome" first appeared in *Crabfat Magazine* (2016).

"We Know It's Rude to Ask" first appeared in Cahoodaloodalaling.com (2016).

"The Reclaiming" first appeared in Cahoodaloodalaling.com (2016).

"Urban Girl Bonds With" first appeared in Rinky Dink Press (2016). Winter Santiaga is the main character in the Urban Lit novel *The Coldest Winter Ever* by Sister Soulja. Bobbi Kristina is the daughter of American musical legend Whitney Huston & Bobby Brown.

The quote from Chapter Three, A Library of Alchemy, is from *The Coldest Winter Ever* (1999) by Sister Soulja.

"The Girl Is from the Hood" first appeared in *3elements Literary Review* (2017).

The quote from Chapter Four, A Name She Buried, is from one of the author's top 5 books, *Sula* (1976), written by the author's favorite author, Toni Morrison.

"Grinding" first appeared in *Door Is Ajar Magazine* (2017).

"We Said *I Love You* But I Think We Were Both Trying to Get the Last Word" first appeared in *(b)OINK* (2019).

"The One Night Stand" first appeared in *Pinch Journal* (2017).

"The Men Want to Know What Is Wrong with Me" first appeared in *A Portrait In Blues,* from Platypus Press (2017).

The quote from Chapter Five, Nothing But End Pieces of Bread, is from *Dust on the Tracks* (1942), an autobiography by Zora Neale Hurston; the author considers Hurston to be the ancestor of her own curiosity & audacity.

"Waste(full)" first appeared in *Tinderbox* (2016) & then again in *Better American Poetry, Vol 2* (2017).

"Atlantis, Discovered" first appeared in *Balkan Press* (2016).

"Hexes for My Exes" first appeared online via Button Poetry (2017).

"Tiffany Haddish as a Recipe for Joy During the Pandemic, & I Watched the *Madam C.J. Walker Story* & Found One Lie I Loved, Or Brown Suga Da Secret" first appeared in *Josephine Quarterly* (2020). The author feels like the title is also the note.

"Orange Is the New Blood" first appeared online via Button Poetry (2018).

"Medium Rare" first appeared in *drunkinamidnightchoir* (2017).

"Urban Girl Is Her Own Nemesis, Or What to Do If" first appeared in *Pinch Journal* (2017).

The quote from Chapter Five, Fortune of Bones, is from writer & queer activist Audre Lorde, delivered at Harvard University, for Malcom X weekend in February 1982. The author considers Lorde to be the ancestor of her own understanding.

"*Fearless* Sounds Like *Fatherless* on the Right Tongue" first appeared in *Gingerbread House* (2017).

"Urban Girl Writes Her City's Name on Tomorrow " first appeared in *Up the Staircase Quarterly* (2016) & then again online via Button Poetry (2018).

"We Are Torn" first appeared in *Chicago Literati* (2015).

The quote from Chapter Seven, What Starts Wail Ends Wail, is from the movie *Crooklyn* (1994), written and directed by Spike Lee. This movie is also in the author's top 5.

"I Met Urbanshee & She Gave Me a Name" first appeared in *Three Drops from a Cauldron: Samhain* (2017).

"It Is Hard to Tell Someone On Fire That You Are Drowning" first appeared in *Hermeneutic Chaos Journal* (2017).

"Another Poem about My Dead Father" first appeared in *Black Napkin Press* (2016).

"Haint Glitter" *Balkan Press* (2018).

"Urban Girl Delicacies// Revenge" first appeared in *Glass Poetry Journal* (2018).

"First of All" first appeared in *Theories of HER* anthology, Mercurial Noodle Press (2017).

"Urbanshee Predicts the Birth of Toni Morrison & Writes Her a Letter", "World in Which the Word *Father* Is Replaced by Hood", and "In Attempts to Bring You Back" first appeared in *The Journal*, The Ohio State University (2022).

About the Author

Siaara Freeman is from Cleveland Ohio, where she is the current Lake Erie Siren & a teaching artist for Center For Arts Inspired Learning and The Westside Community Sisterhood Project in conjunction with the Anisfieldwolf Foundation. She is the 2022 Catapult theater fellow with Cleveland Public Theater. She is a 2021 Premier Playwright fellow recipient with Cleveland Public theater. She is a 2020 WateringHole Manuscript fellow, a 2018 winter tangerine chapbook fellow and a 2018 Poetry Foundation incubator fellow. Her work appears in, *The Offing, BOAAT, Tinderbox, Josephine Quarterly* and elsewhere. She has toured both nationally and internationally. She is the co-founder of Outsiders Queer Midwest Writers Retreat. Chances are she's by a lake, thinking about Toni Morrison and talking to ghosts. In her spare time, she is growing her afro so tall God can use it for a microphone and speak through her.

OTHER BOOKS BY BUTTON POETRY

If you enjoyed this book, please consider checking out some of our others, below. Readers like you allow us to keep broadcasting and publishing. Thank you!

Desireé Dallagiacomo, *SINK*
Dave Harris, *Patricide*
Michael Lee, *The Only Worlds We Know*
Raych Jackson, *Even the Saints Audition*
Brenna Twohy, *Swallowtail*
Porsha Olayiwola, *i shimmer sometimes, too*
Jared Singer, *Forgive Yourself These Tiny Acts of Self-Destruction*
Adam Falkner, *The Willies*
George Abraham, *Birthright*
Omar Holmon, *We Were All Someone Else Yesterday*
Rachel Wiley, *Fat Girl Finishing School*
Bianca Phipps, *crown noble*
Natasha T. Miller, *Butcher*
Kevin Kantor, *Please Come Off-Book*
Ollie Schminkey, *Dead Dad Jokes*
Reagan Myers, *Afterwards*
L.E. Bowman, *What I Learned From the Trees*
Patrick Roche, *A Socially Acceptable Breakdown*
Rachel Wiley, *Revenge Body*
Ebony Stewart, *BloodFresh*
Ebony Stewart, *Home.Girl.Hood.*
Kyle Tran Mhyre, *Not A Lot of Reasons to Sing, but Enough*
Steven Willis, *A Peculiar People*
Topaz Winters, *So, Stranger*
Darius Simpson, *Never Catch Me*
Blythe Baird, *Sweet, Young, & Worried*

Available at buttonpoetry.com/shop and more!

BUTTON POETRY BEST SELLERS

Neil Hilborn, *Our Numbered Days*
Hanif Abdurraqib, *The Crown Ain't Worth Much*
Sabrina Benaim, *Depression & Other Magic Tricks*
Rudy Francisco, *Helium*
Rachel Wiley, *Nothing Is Okay*
Neil Hilborn, *The Future*
Phil Kaye, *Date & Time*
Andrea Gibson, *Lord of the Butterflies*
Blythe Baird, *If My Body Could Speak*
Andrea Gibson, *You Better Be Lightning*

Available at buttonpoetry.com/shop and more!

FORTHCOMING BOOKS BY BUTTON POETRY

Robert Wood Lynn, *How to Maintain Eye Contact*
Usman Hameedi, *Staying Right Here*
Sierra DeMulder, *Ephemera*
Matt Mason, *Rock Stars*
Anita D., *Sitcom Material*
Miya Coleman, *Cotton Mouth*